Pocket Buddha

Tony Morris

MUD
PIE

Mud Pie Books
43 Leckford Road, Oxford OX2 6HY
Registered Co. No. 4405635

ISBN 978-0-9934770-3-4

This book is dedicated
with my deepest respect and gratitude
to the Buddhists of
Leckford Road, Walton and Summertown

Contents

Here and Now

THE BUDDHA WAS born long ago and far away. He grew up in a world without writing, in an ancient civilisation that is no more. The buildings of his childhood, the trees under which he sat in meditation, and the dusty roads down which he once walked have long since vanished from view, buried deep beneath concrete and steel. Even the course of the mighty River Ganges has changed.

And yet something remarkable remains. Over 2,000 years later his words continue to resonate and his teachings continue to inspire. Buddhist statues and shrines, temples and meeting houses can be found in almost every corner of the world. More than 350 million people alive today call themselves 'Buddhist' and look to him as their spiritual forefather. Never has interest in Buddhism been greater or more widespread.

How is it that a man with no home, no money, and no possessions came to be one of the most influential figures in the history of humanity, a giant of world civilisation? Where to begin to tell his remarkable story?

Perhaps with a full moon. For it is said that after a full moon the Buddha arose from meditation, having awakened to the deepest truths of human existence. And it is on the full moon every May that Buddhists today mark this awakening, in a festival known as *Wesak*.

We will never know what he experienced on that world-changing moonlit night over two thousand years ago. We can only imagine ...

So let's begin with the here and now. The Buddha would have approved of that.

Buddhism is the world's fourth largest religion – after Christianity, Islam and Hinduism.[1] It takes many different forms of expression but is generally described in terms of three main traditions.

The Southern, *Theravada*, or 'Elder' tradition prevails in Sri Lanka, Thailand, Burma, Cambodia and Laos. This is the oldest school of Buddhism, claiming both the longest lineage and the earliest collection of scripture – the so-called 'Pali canon'. (Pali is a vernacular form of Sanskrit, close to the language the Buddha would have spoken.)*

The Northern, *Mahayana* or 'Great Vehicle' tradition has its heartland in China, South Korea, Vietnam, Singapore, Taiwan and Japan. Its emphasis is on the compassionate figure of the bodhisattva, a kind of Buddha-in-waiting, whose prime concern is to liberate other people from suffering.

A third, less widespread, Tantric, *Vajrayana* or 'Diamond' tradition is located in Mongolia and in the landlocked countries of the Himalayas – Nepal, Bhutan and Tibet. Vajrayana practices tend to be elaborate and ritualistic in form, with a focus on the cultivation of exceptional, esoteric powers.[2]

There is also an emergent and rapidly evolving Western Buddhist tradition. In fact this seems to be where interest in Buddhism is growing fastest. At a time of increased secularism and suspicion of 'organised religion', with figures for church attendance falling in most parts of the industrialised world, this is a notable phenomenon. It seems to echo the growing popularity of mindfulness training, and it

---

* Note on conventions. Throughout the text, terms are expressed in the form in which they are most commonly found in English, e.g. *Karma* (Sanskrit) rather than *Kamma* (Pali), but *Dukkha* (Pali) rather than *Duhkha* (Sanskrit). Otherwise Sanskrit is the language used.

suggests something about the relevance of Buddhist teachings to the stresses of modern living.

Buddhists are much thinner on the ground in Africa, the Middle East, and in Central and South America, where the evangelical traditions of Christianity and Islam still hold sway. India is also relatively under-represented (which is ironic given that this is where the Buddha spent most of his life), though recent years have seen a revival of interest, inspired by the statesman and social reformer B.R. Ambedkar (1891–1956).

The best-known Buddhist in the world is the Dalai Lama, Tenzin Gyatso, who lives in exile from the land of his birth, Tibet. With his shaved head, twinkling smile and maroon robes, he is most people's idea of what a Buddhist looks like. 'This is my simple religion,' he says. 'There is no need for temples; no need for complicated philosophy. Our own brain, our own heart is our temple; the philosophy is kindness.'

> I believe that every human being has an innate desire for happiness and does not want to suffer. I also believe that the very purpose of life is to experience this happiness.[3]

Thich Nhat Hanh, a Vietnamese monk from the Zen Buddhist tradition, is another figure of world renown, noted especially for his advocacy of peace and mindfulness. Thousands attended the mass meditation he led in Trafalgar Square in 2012. His writings are very popular and his reflections are quoted widely:

Freedom is not given to us by anyone; we have to cultivate it ourselves. It is a daily practice ... No one can prevent you from being aware of each step you take or each breath in and breath out. We need enlightenment not just individually but collectively ... We need to awaken ourselves. We need to practice mindfulness if we want to have a future, if we want to save ourselves and the planet.[4]

The world's most famous female Buddhist is Aung San Suu Kyi. She, like the Dalai Lama, is a Nobel Peace laureate, widely admired for the extraordinary courage and poise she displayed while opposing Burma's military dictatorship (though recently coming under increasing pressure for not being more outspoken in defence of the Rohingya Muslims). Interviewed about Buddhism's role in her life and struggle, she replied:

I have come to respect Buddhist philosophy really deeply during these years of house arrest and detention, when I have had time to medi- tate and to learn to know myself. Buddhism, like any other really good educational process, is all about learning to know yourself, what you are as a human being and what you are capable of as a human being, and that helps a great deal.[5]

There are various Buddhists who are less familiar to a global audience but very well known within their own communities and countries – leaders like Daisaku Ikeda (President of the Soka Gakkai 'value creation' organisation based in Japan); Dr A.T. Ariyaratne (founder of the Sarvodaya Shramadana movement in Sri Lanka – motto: 'We build the road and the road builds us'); Sulak Sivaraksa (Thai social activist and one of the initiators of the International Network of Engaged Buddhists); and Sangharakshita (born Dennis Lingwood, founder of *Triratna*, formerly known as Friends of the Western Buddhist Order) who died in 2018 but whose influence remains profound.

There are also several first-generation Buddhists who are *very* familiar to Western audiences: household names like the actors Richard Gere, Steven Seagal and Orlando Bloom, and the musicians Leonard Cohen (RIP), Tina Turner, Herbie Hancock, k.d.lang, and Philip Glass. In the world of business and innovation, Buddhists don't come any bigger than the late Steve Jobs, charismatic founder of Apple ...[6]

Fame is not, however, the aim of Buddhist

practice! Mention of these celebrities simply illustrates Buddhism's global impact in the age of film and television. As we move further into the digital era it may be that the monks and nuns pictured on YouTube setting fire to themselves in protest at China's policies in Tibet, offer another, more challenging and ultimately more compelling, image of Buddhism in the world today.

In short, Buddhists come in many different shapes and sizes, reflecting the fact that the religious philosophy they follow has a long and remarkably diverse history. But all Buddhists, wherever they live and whatever their particular form of practice, have one thing in common. They all trace their lineage back to a single person called the Buddha. He is their progenitor, their spiritual forefather, the giant upon whose shoulders all Buddhists stand.

1

Life and Legend

BUDDHA IS A TITLE rather than a personal name. It means 'the awakened' or 'enlightened one' and it is one of nearly fifty epithets which feature in the copious writings about his life. Others include: 'all-seeing', 'best of those who can be tamed', 'caravan leader', 'elucidator of meaning', 'foremost of those who can cross', 'shower of the way', 'unconquered conqueror' and 'unsurpassed doctor'.[7]

The name he grew up with was Siddhartha Gautama. Siddhartha means 'one whose goal is accomplished'.[8] Gautama translates as 'best cow' or 'biggest bull' (the term is ungendered), which bears out suggestions that he was born into a wealthy and important family. Siddhartha's father, Shuddhodana, is sometimes (incorrectly as we shall see) described as a king, and Siddhartha as a prince.

Another name by which the Buddha is known, especially in Mahayana Asian countries, is Shakyamuni, the 'Sage of the Shakya clan'. The Shakyas were a tribal people living in the foothills of the Himalayas and along the fertile fringes of the Ganges basin, on the border of what is now northern India and Nepal.[9]

The world into which the Buddha was born, some 2,500 years ago, was changing at a remarkable rate: not just the physical environment, but also the structure and values of society, the way it was organised, who ruled it and how. Towns and cities were starting to spring up across the entire Ganges plain. Money was appearing for the first time. Markets and merchants had begun to proliferate. A new kind of civilisation was coming into being, with new technologies, new trade routes, new means of doing business and new ways of seeing the world.

Traditional rural economies had been caste- or status-bound, tied to the unchanging rhythms of the land, carrying on in much the same way from generation to generation. The rapidly emergent urban centres were very different. These were complex, competitive, cosmopolitan places – bustling and unsettling for many people, but full of opportunity for those with energy, ambition and the ability to adapt.

Every aspect of life seemed to be open to debate in this dynamic context: religion was no exception. The traditional Vedic belief system (*Veda* is Sanskrit for 'knowledge') involved elaborate animal sacrifices and sacred fire ceremonies, presided over by an elite, hereditary class of priests known as Brahmins. To city-dwellers in the new world Vedic rules and rituals were beginning to seem rigid, arcane and outmoded.

The politics of the region were changing fast too. Smaller, clan-based territories such as Shakya, were steadily being incorporated – often by force – into the ambitiously expansionist monarchies of the two biggest states, Kosala and Magadha. This was a time of sporadic warfare and almost constant military tension as these rival neighbouring kingdoms vied for regional supremacy.

The life of the Buddha was thus set against a backdrop of volatility and uncertainty – but also possibility. The philosopher Karl Jaspers has called this the 'Axial Age', and Karen Armstrong writes of 'The Great Transformation' – an era which spawned a number of remarkable philosophers whose chief concern was change and the moral implications of change.

Near-contemporaries of the Buddha included Confucius (551–479 BCE) and Lao Tzu (born c.600 BCE) in China, Socrates (469–399 BCE) and Plato (427–347 BCE) in Greece, Zoroaster (c.628–c.551 BCE) in Persia, and, closest of all in time and space, Vardhamana Mahavira (c.540–c.468 BCE) the founder of Jainism in India. Each of these great teachers responded to the rapid changes taking place around them by developing philosophies which emphasised self-analysis and interior 'depth' rather than 'magical control' and 'external conformity'; inner states of mind rather than outward observances. 'Axial faith', in Karen Armstrong's words, 'put the onus on the individual'.[10] No one, before or since, developed this emphasis further than the Buddha.

Sources

It used to be thought that the Buddha was born 3,000 years ago. The consensus now seems to be five centuries later – somewhere between 563 and 368 BCE. The eminent scholar, Richard Gombrich, has located the date at c.484/5 BCE. He deploys various techniques of textual analysis to arrive at this conclusion, a remarkable feat given the elusive nature of the written sources and the absence of solid archaeology.[11]

It is important from the outset to say something about the sources for what we know of the Buddha's life and teaching. Above all, it is crucial to note that neither the Buddha nor any of his contemporaries could read or write. This was a pre-literate culture. Information was passed down from generation to generation via word of mouth, through storytelling and group recitation. All the documentary evidence about the Buddha's life dates from long after he had died – in some cases many hundreds of years later.

What are called 'Buddhist' texts are not, therefore, transcriptions of what he actually said and did. They are recollections, reports, commentaries, interpretations or treatises by scholars and sages who never met the person to whom they refer. Many are commentaries on commentaries or interpretations of interpretations. Moreover, there is no complete extant narrative account of the Buddha's life. Such a work *may* exist somewhere (who knows how much material has been lost or destroyed over the centuries?) but it has yet to be discovered.

This fact does not of itself undermine the attempt to get at what the Buddha taught. Oral cultures have powerful ways of storing and transmitting collective memories via folk tales, songs and group chanting. Communal recitation ensures that there is no possibility of changes being introduced by a scribe accidentally or on purpose. But it does of course raise questions about the range of 'original' sources scholars have to draw on. Moreover, since the Buddha taught in person rather than by correspondence, it means that there is no single 'definitive' statement of his philosophy to consult. This again may be a strength, for Buddhism has proved itself remarkably flexible, sophisticated and adaptive as a body of thought.

The oldest (and therefore closest to the Buddha in time) surviving body of scripture, is the collection known as the Pali Canon, which dates from the first century BCE. It is a vast accumulation of writings, running to many thousands of printed pages (almost all now available in English and online thanks to the heroic work of the Pali Text Society). It is organised into three 'baskets' (*pitaka*) of material.

The first basket is known as the Vinaya Pitaka. Its focus is on monastic training and discipline. It sets out rules for good conduct and for the proper running of the community of Buddhist monks and nuns. It also features various legends about the Buddha and his followers, which offer useful clues for the would-be biographer.

Second comes the basket of writings known in Pali as the *Sutta Pitaka* – *sutta* (or *sutra* in Sanskrit) being the term for a sermon or discourse attributed to the Buddha. This basket comprises five collections (*nikaya*) arranged mostly by length:

1. The *Digha Nikaya*, an anthology of thirty-four of the longest discourses, together with an account of the Buddha's qualities (*Sampasadaniya*) and the last days of his life (*Mahaparinibbana*).

2. The *Majjhima Nikaya*, an anthology of 152 'middle-length' sutras, featuring a large number of stories about the Buddha, his quest for enlightenment and his early preaching.

3. The *Samyutta Nikaya*, the 'connected discourses' or 'grouped collection' of five series of sutras on topics such as the Eightfold Path.

4. The *Anguttara Nikaya*, the 'collection of numbered sayings'.

5. The *Khuddaka Nikaya*, the 'collection of minor works', which includes popular texts such as the *Dhammapada* – an anthology of the Buddha's epigrams and proverbs; the *Udana* – in which are gathered together some of his maxims; the *Sutta Nipata* which features a number of famous poems and ethical teachings; and the *Jataka* – a series of stories about his previous lifetimes.

The third basket, the Abhidhamma Pitaka, explores philosophical, metaphysical and doctrinal principles and analyses the nature of mind. It is more abstract and includes virtually no personal detail about the Buddha.

In addition to the Pali Canon, there are plentiful sources in other ancient Indian languages, and voluminous works in both Tibetan and Chinese. By comparing and cross-referencing these vast collections it is possible to build up a sense of how the various texts might have evolved over time, how they supplement and corroborate each other – and how they differ.

Inevitably there has been intense scholarly debate about the relative authenticity of the sources, not to mention the quality of their various translations and how they should be interpreted. We cannot say beyond doubt which are the actual words (*Buddhavacana*) of the Buddha. But there does seem to be general acceptance that the voice of a real historical figure is discernible. One commentator talks of 'a consistency and coherence that points to a single original intelligence'. Another discerns a 'distinctive voice'. The great Belgian scholar Etienne Lamotte wrote that 'Buddhism cannot be explained unless we accept that it has its origin in the strong personality of its founder.' And Richard Gombrich is certain that 'one remarkable brain must have been responsible for the basic ideology'.[12]

When it comes to the Buddha's physical appearance, we have few clues. Descriptions of him are idealised. They talk of 'level feet', 'long, slender fingers' and a 'golden-hued' complexion. Among animal attributes he is reported to have had 'thighs like a stag', a 'jaw like a lion', and 'eyelashes like a royal bull'. More unusual among his endowments were the ten-foot aura which enveloped him, the light which supposedly emanated from between his eyebrows, and a fleshy protruberance (*ushnisha*) on the crown of his head, features which at the time were deemed sure signs of exceptional spiritual virtuosity.

Countless images, statues and icons have been made in the centuries since the Buddha's death, some of them on a gigantic scale; but they are all imagined.[13] No one knows what the Buddha really looked like. It is hard to believe that he was as fat as he appears in much iconography given his frugal lifestyle – but we just can't say. As one biographer memorably puts it, when it comes to writing about the Buddha we are hard-pressed to come up with enough 'facts' to fill a single paragraph entry in *Who's Who,* let alone a full-page obituary in the newspapers.[14]

Why this lack of detail? Primarily it is because, unlike modern commentators, the people who recalled the Buddha's memory for posterity were not really interested in the day-to-day minutiae of his existence. What they cared about, far more than analysing his 'personality', was conveying his *message.* The so-called 'Life' of the Buddha is a story with a purpose – a teaching tool. Shaped and rounded by countless retellings, rich with didactic symbolism and allegorical imagery, it is a heroic tale of sacrifice, ordeal and ultimate triumph over adversity, an epic of human suffering and self-realisation. It is, in short, a legend.

Read with the eyes of a mythologist rather than a social historian the traditional narrative of the Buddha's life quickly falls into place.[15] It is an archetypal 'hero's journey' and it centres on a sequence of pivotal events, each framed around a set of stories, arranged into six phases:

1. Birth (childhood and adolescence)
2. Renunciation
3. Quest
4. Awakening
5. Teaching
6. Death

Each of these stages explores a new phase of the Buddha's journey of discovery and encapsulates a different facet of his teaching.

Birth

According to the legend, baby Siddhartha was born into a very well-off household. His father could not have been a king, as described in some texts, since the Shakyas did not operate a system of monarchy; but he was clearly of high-status – a clan elder perhaps.

The place of his birth was a village called Lumbini,

close to the present-day border between India and Nepal. It would have been customary for his mother, Maya, to deliver her first child at the family home in Devadaha some miles away, so it may be that Siddhartha came into the world prematurely. The texts do not comment on this. Nor do they make any psychological play of the fact that Siddhartha never knew his mother – for she died a week after giving birth. He was raised instead by his aunt, Maya's younger sister, Prajapati.

The explanation given in the texts is that, having fulfilled her reproductive destiny, Maya was ready to depart this earth, mission accomplished. But why wait a week? Maternal mortality was common in the ancient world; but to modern eyes it seems obvious that Maya's death *must* have had a profound effect on everyone concerned – her baby, her family, and especially her husband, Siddhartha's father, Shuddhodana. This was his first-born child, his son and heir.

Growing up, Siddhartha must have wondered about the woman who had given birth to him: it would have been only natural. Is it too much to detect in this earliest of traumatic experiences the source of his life-long concern with impermanence, loss and the causes of suffering?[16]

Does Maya's death also offer a clue about Siddhartha's extraordinary upbringing? The legend

tells how he was raised in an ultra-protective environment – doted upon, cossetted and pampered, his
every need catered to. Some tales conjure up images
of a 'pleasure palace' in which only young, healthy
and beautiful people were permitted to attend him,
and where even the flowers were changed daily so
that there should be no evidence of decay.

This is clearly an allegory – or what one biographer
has called an 'evocative fable' – for it is impossible to
believe that anyone could be cocooned in that way.[17]
Another writer sees the palace as a metaphor for a
state of exaggerated psychological 'denial'.[18] In terms
of the narrative structure of the legend its function
is clear: it sets up a dramatic contrast with what
happens next.

Before reaching that point, however, let us pause to
note a brief but significant vignette from Siddhartha's
infancy. It has nothing to do with the special circumstances of his upbringing or the expectations placed
upon him. It features him as an ordinary young child,
and it is important because it offers an interesting
hint of what is to come later, at the climax of the
legend.

The episode in question takes place at the time
of the annual ploughing festival, the ceremonial
initiation of the new agricultural season. Young
Siddhartha is pictured sitting under the cool shade

of a rose-apple tree while all around farmers are tilling the ground, preparing the earth for planting. The boy watches, entranced, as ants work the freshly turned soil, flocks of birds wheel across the cloudless skies and the leaves of the tree shimmer in the sunlight. He hears the bees humming and smells the sweet blossom of the rose-apple. In the midst of all this teeming life he feels effortlessly secure and at peace. And the feeling stays with him ... to be recollected many years later.

Renunciation

The next phase of the legend centres on the parable of the 'Four Signs' or 'Four Sights'. The story goes like this:

As Siddhartha matured, the pleasures of the palace began to pall. The young man itched to find out what life was like away from the confines of his luxurious abode. He was restless and inquisitive.

One day, unable to contain his curiosity any longer, Siddhartha set out in secret to explore the world beyond the palace walls, accompanied only by his loyal servant, Channa.

What he witnessed came as a terrible shock. He saw a very old man, wizened and decrepit.

'Who is this man,' he asked Channa, 'holding a stick, with white hair and shuffling gait, his form bent, his eyes hidden beneath his brows? Why is he like this?'

'That is old age, sir,' replied the charioteer, 'the ravisher of beauty, the ruin of vigour, the cause of sorrow, the destruction of delights.'[19]

Siddhartha was transfixed. He could not get the image out of his mind.

On a second occasion he slipped past the palace guards and ventured out. This time he was confronted by the sight of a very sick person.

'That man with a swollen belly, panting and shaking, his arms hanging loose, his face pale and staring, what is the matter with him?' he asked.

'He is afflicted, sir, with sickness,' replied Channa. 'We are all subject to this evil.'

On a third clandestine expedition Siddhartha witnessed a corpse being carried away for cremation while the dead man's family and friends looked on in grief. Once more he asked Channa to explain.

'That is a dead man, sir, a man who is finished with. His body will be disposed of like mere wood or straw. It is the final end of all beings, no matter who they are.'

The point of the parable is clear. No amount of wealth or privilege could protect Siddhartha from the harsh realities of old age, sickness and death. To be human was to have to confront these raw facts of life – and with them the sufferings of fear, loss and grief.

The fourth 'sight' was to prove decisive in Siddhartha's development. On this occasion the person who caught his eye was a holy man, walking silently from house to house, carrying no possessions other than a bowl – into which people occasionally placed scraps of food.

This man was a shramana (literally 'one who strives') a wandering mendicant who had renounced his home and his family in search of spiritual liberation. Shramanas were an unusual but not uncommon feature of the Ganges civilisation at this time. While others vied for worldly goods, shramanas rejected the values of the city. Some focused on meditation and spent hours seated in focused silence; some emphasised the insights afforded by living close to nature and made the forests their home; some, like the Jains, were extremely ascetic, seeking to cleanse themselves from the taints of the world; some even went naked. Shorn of social constraints and the pressures of convention they were free to roam at will and explore new ways of being ... Rather like the cows which still wander in India's bustling streets, they were a reminder of another rhythm of life, another possibility.

Siddhartha was captivated.

What was it that moved him so much? Perhaps he glimpsed something liberating in the simplicity and spaciousness of the shramanic life, so far removed from the stifling luxury of his own upbringing?

> Living in a house is restricted and cluttered. Going forth is a life wide open.[20]

Perhaps he was chafing under the expectation that he would dutifully follow in his father's footsteps? Or feeling hemmed in by domesticity (he was married by now and his young bride Yasodhara had recently given birth to a baby son, Rahula.) Or perhaps his concerns were more existential. The texts talk of him seeking answers to questions of life, death and the causes of suffering. Whatever their origin, the issues must have been intense to have prompted what happened next. For Siddhartha decided that he, too, must become a shramana, leave home and take up a life on the road.

The power of the legend hinges on this dramatic moment of renunciation. As with all heroic narratives the central character has to respond to a call – a mission if you like – which is greater than his personal circumstances. Siddhartha's decision to give up his old existence (we can imagine the response of his doting family!) encapsulates a timeless truth: that great success is born, more often than not, from great sacrifice.

Thus, as the legend goes, under the cloak of night, Siddhartha rode out through the city gates for the last time, with Channa all the while pleading for him to turn back. Once they had reached the river which marked the edge of Shakya territory, the young man dismounted, exchanged his fine robes for beggar's rags, cut off his long hair at the top-knot, bade farewell to his devoted servant and set off on foot into the distance.

Siddhartha's journey in search of enlightenment had begun.

Quest

His initial quest focused on two people: Alara Kalama and Uddaka Ramaputta were reputed to be the finest spiritual teachers in the land. They taught a set of yogic disciplines and meditation techniques designed to induce profound states of consciousness, far beyond habitual patterns of thought. One account describes entering the 'plane of nothingness', another talks of the further dimension of 'neither perception nor non-perception'.[21]

Siddhartha quickly proved himself an exceptional student – indeed so committed and adept that Uddaka offered to make him a partner in his teaching programme. But the young man declined. The techniques he had learnt did not reach far enough for him: he needed to go beyond mere mental processes. So he set off on his travels once more, this time deep into the forests beyond the margins of society, to a dark and dangerous place where he could test himself to the limit.

It seems that the holy men of yore could perform feats of endurance which are almost impossible to comprehend from the air-conditioned distance of our twenty-first century.[22] Indeed they actively sought out such privations, not simply as masochistic proof of their spiritual commitment but because they understood the power of physical self-mortification to alter mental, emotional and psychic states – to the point where, purified and purged, new forms of consciousness might arise.

Siddhartha did just this. The legend tells how, day after day, he stood motionless beneath the searing heat of the sun and the relentless torrent of the monsoon rains; and how, at night, he slept on cold earth under the stars and open sky. All the while he was at constant threat of attack from wild animals. He ate virtually no food. He stilled his breathing to the point where it was almost imperceptible. 'In this way,' as one writer puts it, Siddhartha 'explored the deepest recesses of physical pain and self-denial.'

> My limbs became like jointed segments of vine-stems, my backside became like a camel's hoof, my spine was like a row of spindles, my ribs were like the rafters of an uncovered barn, my eyes were like the gleam of water at the bottom of a well, my scalp was like a shriveled gourd. I could feel my backbone through my belly, and if I performed my bodily functions I fell over on my face. When I rubbed my limbs the hair came away from my skin.[23]

Even these extreme austerities did not, however, bring the resolution Siddhartha sought. Mortifying the body did not stop his mental strife. On the contrary, it seemed to reinforce it. Time and again he returned to the questions that had set him on his journey in the first place. What was it that could produce in him peace of mind, 'vision ... calm ... direct knowledge ... self-awakening'?[24] The path to enlightenment could not, it seemed, be found via asceticism and self-denial any more than via the worldly pleasures of his adolescent palace or the rigorous mental training he had undertaken with Alara and Uddaka. The answer must lie somewhere else. Siddhartha decided he must leave the forests and return once more to society.

This is another pivotal moment in the legend. Two features stand out.

First, the Buddha's later teachings stressed the importance of a balanced approach, the so-called 'middle way', avoiding the extremes of excessive self-indulgence or self-affliction. He likened psycho-spiritual training to the tuning of a musical instrument: if the strings were too tight the sound would be sharp and shrill; too slack and the notes would be low and flat. An expert musician would find the correct pitch and then adjust all the other strings accordingly so that every sound would be properly calibrated and in harmony.

Second, this was in effect a double renunciation. The small band of shramanas Siddhartha had met during his time in the forests, who had shared his privations and who looked to him as their group leader, could not fathom his decision to leave. To them it felt like a betrayal. Just as he had felt compelled to forsake his family years earlier, Siddhartha once again needed to overcome immense pressure – this time from his peers – in order to remain true to his quest.

Emerging out of the dark world of the forests, Siddhartha headed for the village of Uruvela (modern Bodh Gaya). The legend tells how a young woman called Sujata found him – having at first mistaken him for a tree, he was so black and gnarled. Gently she fed him rice boiled in milk and sweetened with wild honey, the kind of food a mother might give her baby.

As he sat there, slowly regaining strength, Siddhartha's mind went back (in what one writer describes as an 'almost Proustian recollection')[25] to the memory from early childhood of lying in the cool shade of the rose-apple tree, watching the ground being tilled, feeling happy and at ease. No mental or physical strain had been involved, no anguish or yearning. He had simply opened his senses and let the experience flow through him ...

Awakening

And so to the climax of the legend – the point where Siddhartha realises the goal of his quest and becomes the Buddha, the 'awakened one'.

First he bathed in the nearby Neranjara river. Then he calmly seated himself on a bed of soft, freshly cut grass, beneath the spreading canopy of a giant pipal fig tree. Finally, he made a vow, a determination deep in the core of his being, that he would not move on again until he had attained the goal of his searching.

> Skin, sinew, and bone may wither away, flesh and blood may dry up, but without the attainment of complete Enlightenment I shall not leave this seat.[26]

And with that he entered into a profound meditation.

In the spirit of a Bollywood epic, one final battle awaited Siddhartha before he could claim his prize. He had to defeat his old adversary, the so-called 'demon king', Mara.

Mara brings to mind Satan in the Christian story. He is the voice of distraction, negativity and fear – what psychoanalysts today might call a manifestation of Siddhartha's 'shadow'.[27] He appears intermittently throughout the legend, a sinister and slippery presence, taking many different forms and guises. His constant aim is to subvert Siddhartha's quest and he will use every means at his disposal to achieve that end.

First he tried to persuade Siddhartha of the futility of his endeavour, urging him to give up his meditation – to rest and relax. When this failed, Mara sent his three daughters to seduce Siddhartha. Scantily clad dancing girls of exquisite beauty and sensuality, 'some sighed deeply with passion; some undressed slowly before him; some fingered their golden girdles; some swayed their hips like palm trees', all the time whispering sweet nothings in his ear.

Finally, Mara attempted to subjugate him through a series of blood-curdling apparitions, summoning up fearful 'armies of destruction'. 'With spears of copper, flaming swords and cauldrons of boiling oil', the forces of darkness came, 'riding decaying corpses' and 'mad elephants', 'lashing out with hooks and whips and spiked wheels of fire'. It was the stuff of nightmares. But Siddhartha remained calm and impassive. Whatever was hurled at him he turned to 'a rain of flowers, fragrant and soft to the touch'.[28]

Siddhartha had to confront and overcome all of these powerful distractions. The texts state simply that he remained impervious to them. Readers well-versed in meditation might perhaps interpret his response (or lack of it) in terms of mindfulness: once we have become mindful of where, how and why distractions arise – and the crucial fact they are transient – it becomes easier to let them simply pass like clouds, and thus dissipate their power to entangle us. The depth and intensity of Siddhartha's struggle with Mara was the ultimate expression of this process of conscious awareness and triumph over distraction.

When my concentration is immeasurable, my vision is immeasurable, and with immeasurable vision I perceive immeasurable light and see immeasurable form.[29]

Seated beneath the pipal tree, unmoved and implacable in his resolve, Siddhartha's inner journey towards enlightenment continued. What happened next is, of course, impossible to describe. We can only imagine. One account puts it as follows:

He entered into the knowledge of previous exis-tences in the first watch of the night; in the second watch he purified his divine eye; and in the final watch gained an insight into the knowledge of the interdependent causal origins.[30]

Let us try to unpick this description slowly and methodically, for each phase offers important insights not only into the Buddha's experience on that night, but also into what the writers of the legend made of his later teachings.

'In the first watch of the night' (in other words, the first stage of his meditation, between about 6 and 10 p.m.) Siddhartha 'entered into the knowledge of previous existences'. What is meant here by 'previous existences'? We need to look at the issue of rebirth and reincarnation – a belief most people associate with Buddhism, and probably the single most problematic concept from a modern perspective.

First, some historical context. Siddhartha was born into a world in which the idea of rebirth was taken for granted. The seasonal rhythm of the agricultural year was plain for all to see: phases of fertilisation and growth followed by periods of shedding and decay, regeneration and new growth. Human existence was regarded similarly, as a constant round of birth, death and rebirth. According to the prevailing Vedic view, 'individual existences were thought of like pearls on a necklace – each one separate but strung together in an endless series'.[31] This was the process referred to in the texts as *samsara*, which literally translates as 'flowing on' or 'keeping going continuously'.

Is this a viable concept from a modern perspective? The first law of thermodynamics (the law relating to the conservation of energy) states that energy can never disappear: it simply continues in a different form – so there is no scientific objection to the notion of the constant flow of life. The debate therefore centres on what precise form human 'rebirth' might take. Here the different schools of Buddhism vary considerably.

Is belief in some form of physical rebirth essential

if one is to call oneself a Buddhist? Yes – according to traditional scholarship: it is the only logical conclusion to draw if the law of cause and effect is to hold true.[32] Not necessarily – according to commentators like Stephen Batchelor, who argues that 'rebirth' is much more usefully conceived in metaphorical, present-life terms.[33]

Whenever the Buddha was asked what happens after we die, he deflected the question, saying it was not a fruitful line of enquiry: it wasn't – one of his favourite adjectives – 'skilful' (*upaya-kaushalya*). First, it went beyond the realm of normal human consciousness so no answer to the question could be meaningful. Second, it was a distraction from the key task of ending suffering in the here and now. Third, as he pointed out wryly, we would find out for ourselves soon enough!

Listen – if you had just been shot by a poison-tipped arrow, you wouldn't be standing there asking me, 'Who fired it? What did they look like? Where did they come from?' ... You'd be saying: 'Help! Get this arrow out! Quick!'[34]

Let us return to the pipal tree. The legend tells how, as he entered deeper and deeper into meditation, Siddhartha sensed an ever more profound awareness of the continuity of life. He began to experience his existence stretching back deep into the distant past. He reached the point where he could actually picture himself being reborn through countless incarnations. He saw his 'entire life', as it were, generation after generation, coming into being, growing, ageing, declining, dying ... and coming into being again:

> There I had such a name, belonged to such a clan, had such an appearance. Such was my food, such my experience of pleasure and pain, such the end of my life. Passing away from that state, I re-arose there. There too I had such a name, belonged to such a clan, had such an appearance. Such was my food, such my experience of pleasure and pain, such the end of my life. Passing away from that state, I re-arose here. Thus I remembered my manifold past lives in their modes and details.[35]

In this constant round of birth and death did Siddhartha experience sadness at the transience of human existence, or simply awareness of its true nature? Was he seeking to put an end to the non-stop cycle of samsara because it involved so much loss and anguish? Or was he beginning to reimagine the very nature of what we call suffering and the reasons we experience unhappiness?

❖ ❖ ❖

In the 'second watch' (between approximately 10 p.m. and 2 a.m.) Siddhartha is said to have 'purified his divine eye'. This is an odd expression, because he never claimed god-like or super-human status. Indeed, the whole premise of Buddhism is that the capacity for awakening is inherent in all human beings, whoever they are and wherever they come from. What, then, are we to make of this passage?

According to most interpretations it expresses the moral dimension to causation. Everything in the world comes about as the result of something else: it has a cause. Or, rather, causes – for there are myriad conditions and causes – and thus myriad effects. Causes and effects. Effects and causes. Everything is linked. Everything is interconnected:

When this exists, that comes to be. With the arising of this, that arises. When this does not exist, that does not come to be. With the cessation of this, that ceases.[36]

What Siddhartha observed in the second watch of the night was the connection between what we do in the present and what we experience in the future. He realised how we are shaped by the thoughts we think, the words we speak and the actions we take. This is the working through of what is called karma and it has profound implications for how the Buddha later came to frame his explanation of ethics.

Karma is a Sanskrit word – and it is much misunderstood. It translates, literally, as 'action'; but the way it has come into everyday Western usage gives it an inflection akin to 'fate'. People are sometimes heard to complain that it's their 'karma' to get a low-paid job, or to be rejected in a relationship. (Notice, incidentally, how often it is 'bad' rather than 'good' karma – which perhaps says something about the link between pessimism and passivity.) In fact, there is nothing fatalistic about karma whatsoever – precisely the opposite. The whole of Buddhist teaching rests on the premise that we are *not* victims of some arbitrary and impersonal fate. We can be the architects of our future rather than the prisoners of our past. We can shape our destiny.

By extending the traditional, fixed Brahminical teaching about causation and rebirth into a philosophy of dynamic personal responsibility for minute-to-minute thought, word and deed, the Buddha was pointing to a radical new possibility. Change the way we think about the world and we change the way we see it. Change the way we see it and we change the way we act. Change the way we act and we change the world itself.

The kind of seed sown
Will produce that kind of fruit.
Those who do good will reap good results.
Those who do evil will reap evil results.
If you carefully plant a good seed,
You will joyfully gather good fruit.[37]

The workings of karma may sometimes appear mysterious, especially when based on unconscious or subconscious influences in our lives, but they are never random. They are patterned, specific and consequential – 'conditioned', to use the Buddhist term. They operate according to the strict law of cause and effect. Acts based on greed, cruelty and foolishness not only harm other people but also cause us long-term suffering at a deep level. Kind and wholesome (*kushala*) acts based on goodwill, generosity and compassionate understanding make for happiness all round.

Hence, 'every instant of experience is morally significant and offers an opportunity for liberation', both individually and collectively.[38] Put another way: if human beings are creatures of habit, which habits work well, and which do not? It is up to us to choose wisely because everything we think, say or do has an impact on the wellbeing of others and shapes the person we become.

Sow an act, reap a habit; sow a habit, reap a character; sow a character, reap a destiny.[39]

Developing insight into the operation of karma – purifying our 'divine eye' is, therefore, one of the keys to awakening. This is what Siddhartha saw so clearly as he sat in meditation beneath the pipal tree on that momentous moonlit night.

❖   ❖   ❖

'In the final watch [Siddhartha] gained an insight into the knowledge of the interdependent causal origins.'[40] Once again the language is compressed and complex. The idea behind it is, however, relatively straightforward. In this third phase of his deepening meditation Siddhartha synthesised the two preceding insights. He observed the continuum of past, present and future, and he experienced the connectedness of all aspects of existence throughout time and space.

This is the principle which came to be known as 'dependent origination', 'co-arising' or 'conditioned genesis' (*pratitya-samutpada*), a remarkably rich and profound concept which was elaborated by later Buddhist scholars into a complex analysis of the interwoven components of existence – the twelve links (*nidanas*) in the great chain of being, the twelve spokes in the wheel of life, and beyond that the idea of 'three thousand possibilities in a single life-moment'.[41]

In essence (though it is of course impossible to convey in mere prose) Siddhartha experienced, at his very core what Mahayana Buddhists might call the fundamental 'interbeing' of life in all its forms.[42]

> He ... entered the great ocean of life in which all distinctions of mind and body, self and environment are entirely eliminated ... He experienced a dynamic, moment-to-moment sense of his own being and all phenomena around him undergoing formation and disintegration in perfect harmony ... In other words, he grasped the eternal truth that the rhythm of life supported, at the core, his own being and all phenomena ... He awakened to this mystic reality of life in which all things of the universe including human life interrelate, permeate and influence one another.[43]

Siddhartha had 'woken up' to the deepest truth of human existence. He had become a Buddha.

Opening his eyes, he experienced the world afresh – the river gently slipping by, the canopy of leaves above him shimmering in the sun, the grasses rustling at the water's edge, the sounds of birdsong, the smells of the river mud. He sensed the strangeness and sheer wonder of being alive, and for a long time he simply sat there and drank it all in, resting in the profundity of what he had realised.[44]

The legend relates that he remained in Gaya for several weeks. Exhausted after all the ordeals of his quest, and at the same time exhilarated by his point of arrival, he was perhaps weighing up whether or not to go back home to his Shakya people and family.

But his spiritual task was not yet complete. The insights he had attained after so much struggle demanded to be shared so that future generations could benefit from what he had learnt and experienced. This was the compassionate thing to do.[45] And so it was that he embarked on a second journey, one that was to last the remainder of his lifetime, some forty-five years. Siddhartha the seeker became Buddha the teacher.

2

Teaching

THE BUDDHA WAS, by all accounts, an exceptional teacher. He seemed able to respond in a
unique and personal way to everyone who approached
him, and he had a remarkable gift for rapport:

> I matched my appearance to their appearance, I
> matched the sound of my voice to the sound of
> theirs, and I instructed them with talk about the
> teaching, encouraging, enthusing and inspiring
> them.[46]

Kings, nobles, outlaws, merchants, children, pros-
titutes, 'untouchables', even murderers: whoever
came to him and whatever their station in life, he
met them as equals. From the many stories told in
the sutras it is clear that he had an almost uncanny
ability to look into their questions and penetrate to
the core of what was being asked of him. Like a sensi-
tive doctor he seemed able to see every symptom in
context and quickly get to the heart of the malaise.

In one famous story he was approached by a young mother, Kisa Gautami, clutching the corpse of her small child. Distraught with grief, she pleaded with the Buddha to bring her baby son back to life. This was clearly impossible. But, rather than confront Kisa with the unpalatable truth, the Buddha agreed to her request provided she fulfil a simple task – to bring him some mustard seeds. There was one condition, however: the seeds had to come from a household where no death had taken place.

Kisa readily agreed and set off determinedly. The first household she called at gave her the mustard seeds; but when she asked if anyone in the family had died they admitted that the grandmother had passed away recently. So Kisa moved on. At the next household she asked the same question. This time it was a husband who had died. At the third household it was an uncle; at the fourth an aunt. And so on. Kisa came to realise that death had come to every family in the village and that her bereavement was not unique. This understanding helped to ease her grief and she was eventually able to bury her son's body in peace.

In another story the Buddha managed to convert a terrifying mass murderer. The name of the man was Angulimala, meaning 'finger necklace', so called because when he killed his victims he cut off their fingers and strung them into a gruesome garland which he wore round his neck. One day Angulimala encountered the Buddha walking slowly and mindfully in the forest. Gleefully he drew his bloodstained sword and began to chase after his prey. But, no matter how fast he ran, he could not catch up with the Buddha. In frustration he called out: 'Monk, stop! Stop! Stand still!'

The Buddha turned round calmly and looked into the eyes of his would-be assassin. 'I am still – why don't you stop too?' he said. 'What do you mean?' asked the agitated Angulimala. 'I am still because I have stopped harming living beings,' said the Buddha. 'You are not still because you keep on killing.'

The murderer saw in an instant the wretchedness of his life, broke down and let his sword drop to the ground, whereupon the Buddha agreed to allow him to become a follower and to take on a new identity and a new name – Ahimsaka, meaning 'harmless'.

Like Socrates, the 'father of Western philosophy', the Buddha seems to have had a love of dialogue and a gift for gentle but incisive interrogation. He had two favourite techniques. The first was to turn questions back onto his questioners, to get them to explore what it was they were really asking. The second was to take a well-known phrase or metaphor and use it in a different way, infusing it with new meaning. For instance, he often transposed martial imagery into the inner battle of spiritual development:

Though one should conquer thousands upon thousands of men, he who conquers himself is truly the greatest in battle.

He who holds back rising anger checks a whirling chariot, him I call a real charioteer; other people are merely holding the reins.[47]

Clearly and without a trace of condescension, he seemed able to accompany his questioners on a journey of enquiry until they had reached the answer for themselves. It was essential that they *did* find the answers for themselves, not just take him at his word. The Buddha's constant injunction was not to accept things at face value or because someone in authority had made a pronouncement, but to challenge, investigate and experiment, to test and pursue a line of enquiry until one knew it to be true in the depth of one's being. His most famous articulation of this came in a discourse he delivered to the people of the Kalama clan:

Do not go upon what has been acquired by repeated hearing,
nor upon tradition,

nor upon rumour,
nor upon what is in a scripture,
nor upon surmise,
nor upon an axiom,
nor upon specious reasoning,
nor upon a bias towards a notion that has been
pondered over,
nor upon another's seeming ability,
nor upon the consideration, "The monk is our
teacher."[48]

For the Buddha, true knowledge could not be
derived from second-hand explanation, divine revelation, holy writ or abstract theory. It had to be
grounded in direct personal experience: 'That which
you affirm [must be] that which you have realised,
seen, known for yourself.'[49]

Sometimes he had no need for words at all. In the
case of the famous Flower Teaching which lies at the
heart of the Zen tradition, the Buddha is said simply
to have held up a white lotus flower and smiled. His
aim was to get his followers to look at it – really look
at it – and appreciate its sublime wonder, far beyond
the capacity of words to encapsulate.[50]

This radical emphasis on personal insight and
direct experience goes to the heart of the Buddha's
method. He was not anti-intellectual (the Buddhist

tradition has furnished some of the world's most sophisticated and refined scholarship). His point was that the intellect has limitations. Used wisely, it could be powerful tool; wrongly applied it could be dangerously deceptive. Knowledge needed to be grounded in practice not theory. What the Buddha taught was, at its heart, a 'philosophy of experience'.[51]

As to the application of knowledge, his approach was equally pragmatic. He had little time for complex speculation or mystification. The proper test of a teaching was whether or not it worked. Did it lead to self-transformation and deeper understanding? Did it make one wiser, more compassionate, more 'skilful' – that word again – in the art of living?

This rigorously empirical approach to the great questions of life, based on honesty, personal experience, insight, sincere effort and skill, was a hallmark of the Buddha's brilliance and originality. In keeping with this spirit of eternally fresh enquiry he urged his followers not to become fixated on any single version of 'reality'. 'Clinging to views' was dangerous, he suggested, for it could easily lead to dogmatism, and from there to dispute and discord.

In one well-known story from the Pali Canon the Buddha instanced a group of blind men being asked to describe an elephant. One man felt the leg and concluded that the mystery object was a tree.

Another felt its ear and proclaimed it a basket. A third felt its trunk and was certain it was a plough. A fourth interpreted its tusks as a ploughshare. A fifth grabbed its tail and declared he was holding a brush – and so on. Each described a different object, having felt only part of the whole animal. For the Buddha, truth was holistic, never partial.

Indeed, the Buddha taught that even his own words were to be seen and applied in context. He likened his teachings to a raft. The purpose of a raft was to cross a river. Having reached the bank on the other side, the raft should be put down. To carry on dragging it around would be considered foolish. In other words, his teaching was not an end in itself but an expedient means. One must never mistake a hand pointing to the moon for an understanding of the moon itself.

In this and countless other teachings emphasising the fundamental contingency of time, place and context, the Buddha demonstrated his genius as one of the most original and radical teachers of all time.

Change

The Buddha's core ethical concern was to remove suffering. His prime metaphysical concern, therefore, was to demonstrate the conditions under which suffering arose. Underpinning all the Buddha's teachings is a philosophy of change. It has three facets.

First, change over time: impermanence. Nothing lasts for ever. Nothing is fixed. In-breath, out-breath, day, night, summer, winter: the world is in a state of constant flux. Some changes are immediately obvious – flickering flames, clouds shifting across the sky. Some changes become evident over time – the length of one's hair, the depth of foliage on a tree. Some changes are imperceptible to the human eye – the movement of a tectonic plate, the spinning of the earth upon its access. But, visible or not, everything is changing all of the time. And everything that exists will sooner or later disappear. Nothing in our solar system is eternal. Indeed, the very sun at its heart will one day be gone. The Sanskrit word for this concept of impermanence is *anitya*.

Second, change in content: non-substantiality.[52] Nothing is as it seems on the surface. Under a microscope even the most apparently solid objects can be seen to be made up of multiple smaller components – granules, molecules, sub-atomic particles and so on. These miniscule fragments coalesce in such a way as to convey the impression of fixity. But what has been put together will eventually move apart. This is what is meant by the Buddhist teaching that all things are 'conditioned' or 'composite'.

In human terms this means subjectivity. In the words of the proverb (often attributed to the Buddha's near contemporary, the Greek philosopher Heraclitus) we cannot step in the same river twice. This is doubly true. Not only is the river changing all the time: we are changing all the time too. When we look at an old photograph there is clearly a resemblance to the person we are now; but it isn't the 'same old me' because the old me and the new me are not identical. And the closer we look, the more we will search in vain for an essence, a spirit, a 'soul' that is fixed or solid or separate or eternal. The photograph is pixelated and the subject of the photograph is also a composite. This is the concept of 'no fixed self'. The Sanskrit term is *anatman*.

Third, change in relationship: interdependence. Nothing is separate. Nothing happens in isolation. You cannot have an 'us' without a 'them' or an observation without an observer. Change in one area causes change in others – the so-called 'butterfly effect'. Everything in the known universe is inter-connected throughout space and time. The Buddha's teachings ultimately flowed from this insight, and it was when he awoke to its fullest implications that he became truly enlightened.

Four Noble Truths

Numbers have significance in most spiritual traditions – the number three in particular – and Eastern religions are especially fond of them.[53]

Being a consummate teacher, the Buddha was always trying to tailor what he said to the needs of his audience. He therefore devised a set of simple formulae which encapsulated the essence of his teaching. A small set of numbers was a good prompt. Numbers also helped his teachings to be remembered and transmitted down the generations. It may well be – in fact it is almost certain – that when the teachings were eventually committed to writing they were packaged and refined even more neatly than he expressed them at the time.

The best known of the Buddha's teachings are the Four Noble or Great Truths and the Eightfold Noble Path. According to tradition these were first outlined in a teaching he gave shortly after his enlightenment to his former companions from the forest. The story goes that he caught up with them in a deer park called Isipatana (close to the modern holy city of Benares). At first they were hesitant to greet him, still feeling resentful that he had abandoned them a few weeks earlier. But eventually they relented and all sat down together, whereupon the Buddha began to recount the events of the preceding weeks and the realisations he had come to under the pipal tree in Gaya.

The teaching he gave is known as the Dharma Chakra Pravartana Sutra – 'Setting in Motion the Wheel of the Law'. In it he outlined a clear and straightforward approach to spiritual wellbeing. Like a doctor, he set out (1) the problem, (2) the cause, (3) the diagnosis and (4) the prescription:

1. The truth of suffering.
2. The truth of the craving which causes suffering.
3. The truth that craving can cease, and suffering with it.
4. The way craving and suffering can be made to cease through cultivation of the right path in life.

The essence of the first truth is that life is *dukkha*. This word is notoriously difficult to translate.[54] It has connotations of being 'out of kilter' or 'in a bad place'. The traditional rendering of it as 'suffering' can sometimes sound harsh and pessimistic. 'Stress' may be a better way of putting it. One commentator writes of 'inadequacy, insubstantiality, incompleteness, uncontrollability ... the fundamental imperfection-cum-impermanence ... which is inherent in all experience.'[55]

But dukkha isn't just about the hard facts of everyday life. It points to a much deeper level of existential angst. The knowledge that we are going to grow old, get ill and eventually die can be profoundly unsettling. No one will escape this process; no one is immune to the challenge of this dread realisation. All human beings are destined to suffer at some point in their lives.[56]

> Now this, monks, is the noble truth of stress: Birth is stressful, aging is stressful, death is stressful; sorrow, lamentation, pain, distress, and despair are stressful; association with the unbeloved is stressful, separation from the loved is stressful, not getting what is wanted is stressful. In short, [life is] stressful.[57]

The Second Noble Truth asserts that there is a reason for this stressful state of affairs. It 'arises' (the term most often used in translations) as the result of a set of circumstances or conditions. Why? What is it that makes us stressed, anxious and unhappy? What causes us to suffer? The Buddha identified what he called 'three poisons' – greed, hatred and delusion.

Greed

Greed makes us grasping. It tells us that we need

more food, more drink, more wealth, more power, more fame. It tries to convince us that getting these will make us feel better. But it almost certainly won't. For the nature of greed is that it is never satisfied. It will always seek out new things to lust after.

Greed makes us anxious about what we have as well as what we don't have. We attract the 'soul mate' then worry how to cling on to them; we get the dream job and become fearful of losing it; after the jackpot win comes the stress over what to do with the money. And so it goes on ... We are condemned to spend our lives walking what some economists have called the 'treadmill of desire'.[58]

Greed has a further propensity – to get ever more intense, so that our wants gradually come to feel like 'needs'. If we aren't vigilant we may find ourselves hooked, addicted, prisoners to our cravings. The word for craving is *trishna* in Sanskrit, *tanha* in Pali. It goes to the heart of the Second Noble Truth.

> Craving is repetitive, it wallows in attachment and greed, obsessively indulging in this and that: craving for stimulation, craving for existence, craving for non-existence.[59]

(Note, incidentally, the reference to the craving for 'non-existence' as a greedy impulse. This is the instinct to destroy, to sabotage and to self-harm – which can also become perversely addictive.)

Craving is not confined to sensual pleasures. At a deeper level we crave certainty and hold fast to increasingly rigid views of our place in the world: 'Attachment to views, adherence to views, fixation on views, addiction to views, obsession with views, clinging firmly to views.'[60]

How then did the Buddha suggest we overcome this poison of greed and craving? First, we need to see it clearly for what it is, recognise the ways it operates and the tricks it plays in order to keep us in its thrall. We need to learn to break the identification between who we are and what we crave. 'Every consciousness is to be seen as it actually is with right discernment as: "This is not mine. This is not my self. This is not what I am."'[61]

Second, we need to refocus. Like a greedy child whose hand is jammed in a jar of sweets, we need to let go in order to release ourselves. Or, like an alcoholic whose thirst can never be quenched by drinking more liquor, we need to change what we are consuming into something healthier.

Finally, we need to reverse this greedy, clinging process which seems to bind us in its grip. We can begin to do this by practising not merely detachment from craving, but positive, active generosity:

opening up the tight, grasping sense of self, until it has become transformed into an expansive desire for the wellbeing and happiness of everyone. Loving-kindness (*maitri*), compassion *(karuna)*, sympathetic joy (*mudita*) and equanimity (*upeksa*) – what the Buddha called the four 'boundless', 'immeasurable' or sublime states: these qualities are the opposite of greed and it is by cultivating them that we 'turn poison into medicine'.[62]

Hatred

Hatred is another state of mind that has the capacity to be all-consuming and highly destructive. Where does this potentially deadly poison come from?

The Buddha taught that it arises as a result of 'Self' – or what we might nowadays call 'Ego'. The Self is a tyrant. It insists on being right. Often in the face of conflicting evidence it clutches onto a compulsively Self-serving version of events. It places itSelf at the centre of every story, the sun around which everything else must orbit. We are, the Buddha says, driven by Self-importance.

The Self is bent on a mission to dominate and aggrandise – so if other Selves get in the way conflict is inevitable. Any threat to the Self's demand for omnipotence will trigger a counter-assertion. The culmination is often physical and verbal violence. Sometimes these aggressive feelings may be turned inward. Depression is often fuelled by feelings of Self-loathing. Suicide is the ultimate attempt at Self-destruction.

The irony of course is that, according to the Buddha, we are not the same as what we call 'ourSelf'. We have been psychologically hijacked. The Buddhist solution is to see hatred for what it really is – a state of deluded and damaging Self-obsession. We need to challenge and face down this tyrant. The Self has to be 'dethrone(d) ... from the centre of [its] own private universe'.[63] 'Self–forgetting' is the phrase used by Peter Conradi in his wonderful book, *Going Buddhist*.[64]

Ignorance

Ignorance – 'foolishness', 'stupidity' or 'delusion' as it is sometimes expressed – is by definition the most difficult of the three poisons to identify, because one is too deluded to recognise how deluded one is! In a state of delusion, no matter how noble our stated aims, the effect of our actions is to make the suffering worse. We become unbalanced and ultimately destructive, because we are, quite simply, out of touch with reality.

Thinking the impermanent is permanent, that is ignorance. Thinking there is a self when there is not, that is ignorance. From ignorance is born greed, anger, fear, jealousy, and countless other sufferings. The path of liberation is the path of looking deeply at things in order to truly realise the nature of impermanence, the absence of a separate self, and the interdependence of all things. This path is the path which overcomes ignorance. Once ignorance is overcome, suffering is transcended. That is true liberation.[65]

How do we break this cycle of ignorance, and the suffering that goes with it? How do we step off this treadmill, this relentless samsara? The Third Noble Truth points out that if dukkha has a cause, then there must logically be a way of obviating that cause and of bringing about a cessation (*nirodha*) to suffering. Let us start, the Buddha says, by looking inside ourselves and finding out more about what is really going on.

Awareness

What is the source of these three poisons – greed, hatred, ignorance? Where do they come from? They arise, the Buddha teaches, in the mind. They are aspects of human consciousness.[66] To understand them properly we therefore need to observe how our mind works, and how it so often leads us astray.

The greedy mind craves constant gratification. The selfish mind sees difference as threatening rather than enriching. The deluded mind prefers to remain blinkered rather than make the effort to expand itself. More than that, the mind cannot seem to keep still. Permanently restless, it is constantly demanding something new to grab its attention. Like a small child tugging at its mother's sleeve, the mind is always trying to drag our focus away from the present moment.

When it does this we lose the ability to be fully conscious, fully present in the here and now. Our thoughts become fragmented and scattered. We spend more and more time looking over our shoulder, fretting about past regrets, or gazing out towards the far-distant horizon and worrying about an imagined future.

In one memorable teaching the Buddha likens us to dogs on a leash tied firmly to a pillar. We chase round and round, going nowhere, never freeing ourselves from what it is that drives us.[67] If we want to stop going round in circles we need to start our journey of liberation by looking in the right place. We have to start with the here and now and focus on what is at the centre of our existence.

A variant of this teaching is expressed in the parable of the Jewel in the Robe.

Once upon a time there lived a man who had, as a friend, a rich public servant. One day the man called on his rich friend, who entertained him with food and wine. He became completely inebriated and fell asleep. The rich man had to set out on a journey involving urgent public business. He wanted to give his friend a ... jewel ... But his friend was fast asleep. Finding no other alternative, he sewed the precious gem into the hem of his sleeping friend's robe. The man awoke to find his friend gone, completely unaware of the jewel ... Before long, he sank into poverty, wandering through many countries and experiencing many hardships. After many years, now reduced to sheer want, he once again encountered his old friend. The rich man, surprised at his condition, told him about the gift he had given him, and the man learned for the first time that he had possessed the priceless jewel all along.[68]

In other words we already possess the means to prevent suffering: we have the precious gem of awareness. It is a fundamental aspect of what the Mayahana tradition refers to as our 'Buddha nature' (*tathagatagarbha*), the capacity for enlightenment inherent in all human beings.

We have the resources at our disposal, but we have to wake up and activate them. There is work to do (Stephen Batchelor has reframed the Truths as Four Noble Tasks).[69] Far from being passive, as it is commonly depicted, Buddhism enjoins us to *act*.

First, we need to appreciate the urgency of the job at hand by facing up to the transitory nature of existence. Second, we need to understand the law of cause and effect, and the interrelationship of thought, word and deed. Third, we need to cultivate our ability to pay attention to what is really going on in the mind, the body and the environment, so that we can *respond* afresh to new situations rather than *react* mindlessly according to the pattern of our accumulated habits or karma.

Above all we need to stop throwing petrol on the fire.

All is burning, Monks. And what is the all that is burning? The eye is burning ... The ear is burning ... The nose is burning ... The tongue is burning ... The body is burning. The mind is burning, ideas are burning, stimulation of the mind is burning; and whatever ... feeling that comes about conditioned by stimulation of the mind, that, too, is burning.

Burning by what? I say it is burning with the fire of greed, the fire of hatred, the fire of delusion; burning with birth, with old age, with death, with grief, with lamentation, with pain, with sorrow, with despair.[70]

Fire imagery occurs frequently in the Buddha's teaching. His audience would have got the allusion instantly, for the Brahmins made great use of fire in their Vedic rituals. By extending the metaphor into the psychological realm the Buddha was seeking to shift the focus from magical practice and external propitiation towards private intention and personal responsibility – in other words, the impulses that drive thinking and behaviour. Fire is a thing; combustion is a process.

How do we put an end to this conflagration? By removing the fuel and developing the necessary psychological skills to cool the inflamed mind. Thus the ground is cleared for the Buddha to introduce the fourth of his Noble Truths, the teaching of the Eightfold Path.

The Eightfold Path

The Buddha identified eight areas of our life which require attention if we want to become more enlightened. His reference to a path (*marga*) suggests a step-by-step process, but Buddhist models are rarely linear. All eight aspects are interconnected and need to be kept in balance with each other at all times.

Balance was a central theme of the Buddha's teaching. He often spoke of the 'middle way' and of the need to avoid extremes. Having personally experienced both great wealth and great privation he spoke with considerable authority when it came to discussions about material living. On a spiritual level his teaching steered a path between the 'eternalist' views of the Brahmins with their notion of an indestructible essence or *atman*, and the 'nihilist' views of some Shramanic teachers who denied any possibility of continuity. We should not, however, think of the middle way as static or fixed, like an arithmetic average or mean. As with all Buddhist models, it is a position of dynamic, ever-changing equilibrium and poised awareness – which is why the concept has given rise to many varying interpretations according to the emphases of different Buddhist schools.

Finding the middle way is often very difficult. Witness the world around us with its simultaneous epidemics of obesity and starvation. The same asymmetry operates at an individual level: people seem to suffer stress either as a result of having no job and nothing to do, or from being too busy and 'time poor'. It is often difficult to balance the demands of work and family, or to maintain focus when there are so many gadgets to distract us. We rarely seem to give ourselves permission to appreciate, let alone cultivate, our lives.

The eight components of the path can be summarised as follows:

Right View – seeing the true nature of reality, which is transient and bound by the law of cause and effect.

Right Intention – making a serious commitment to develop the qualities of wisdom and generosity, courage and compassion, together with a corresponding determination not to be distracted from the path.

Right Speech – telling the truth with sensitivity, speaking in a way which doesn't hurt or divide others, avoiding gossip and idle chatter.

Right Action – abstaining from harmful behaviour such as killing, stealing, or abusing sensual pleasures.

Right Livelihood – not participating in an occupation which causes harm to others.

Right Effort – gaining control of one's thoughts, restraining negative states of mind and replacing them with positive ones.

Right Mindfulness – cultivating constant and consistent awareness of one's body, feelings, mental states, and thoughts.

Right Concentration – developing deep levels of calm and insight through various techniques which concentrate the mind and integrate the personality.

The word 'right' is interesting because 'right' is never specifically prescribed: it is contextual. 'Appropriate' might be a better term. The Buddha did not say, 'This is the only way for all people to behave at all times and in all places.' He posed a challenge: to work out what is relevant, valuable and effective in any given situation. There *is* a right and appropriate thing to do, but we will only know it when we try it and it works. Once more there is a call to action implicit in his words. A path only becomes meaningful in the process of using it. We continuously remake it afresh as we walk it.

The eight components of the Way are traditionally organised into three main categories: *Prajna*, meaning wisdom or discernment – comprising Right View and Right Intention; *Shila*, usually translated as ethics, virtue or good conduct – including Right Speech, Right Action and Right Livelihood; and *Samadhi* or concentration – incorporating Right Effort, Right

Mindfulness and Right Meditation. Each of these informs the other.

> Concentration that is invested with good conduct is of great fruit and of great benefit ... wisdom that is invested with concentration is of great fruit and of great benefit ... the mind that is invested with wisdom is fully released from the taints of craving and ignorance.[71]

It would be possible to write a book on any of the eight components. Here let us concentrate briefly on two: Right Intention and Right Meditation – the first because it goes to the ethical heart of the Buddha's teaching, the second (which I've called meditation although it is also somewhat confusingly referred to as concentration) because it is the spiritual practice most commonly associated with Buddhism in the world today.

Right Intention

One of the Buddha's greatest contributions to human understanding was his delineation of the conscious and unconscious impulses which inform how we behave. He taught that thought and deed are insepa-rable, and he emphasised that physical actions are fuelled by the mental processes behind them. Indeed, he went so far as to say, 'By action (*karma*) I mean intention (*cetana*).' It could be argued that the core aim of Buddhist training is to understand, refine and purify the quality of intention.

> We are what we think
> Having become what we thought
> Like a wheel that follows a cart-pulling ox
> Sorrow follows an evil thought.
>
> And joy follows a pure thought,
> Like a shadow faithfully tailing a man.
> We are what we think,
> Having become what we thought.[72]

In essence, the Buddha analysed human behaviour in the way a modern psychologist might, identifying the motives and drives ('drive' is a very useful term as it suggests 'we' are not always in control) which lead us to respond in particular ways. As one commentator memorably puts it, 'Buddhism sees human beings as verbs rather than nouns.'[73]

Making intention, which had hitherto been regarded as an internal, private matter, the ultimate criterion for judging ethical value, was, in the words of Richard Gombrich, 'utterly radical and new', in fact nothing less than 'a turning point in the history of civilisation'.[74] 'Revolutionary' is the adjective used by Karen Armstrong, for the Buddha's teaching 'deepened the entire question of morality, which was now located in the mind and heart and could not merely be a matter of outward behaviour'.[75]

It follows, according to Buddhist logic, that a capacity for empathy is essential if we are to behave ethically – i.e. with the Right Intention. It also follows that Right Intention arises from Right View because we recognise that another person's happiness is not separable from our own. We are all connected. Hence the ethical injunction to cultivate compassion, which literally means 'fellow-feeling'.

'If you want others to be happy practice compassion. If *you* want to be happy, practice compassion,' writes the Dalai Lama.[76] The Buddha taught that all living beings are worthy of respect and that everyone possesses the capacity for enlightenment.[77] The goal of Buddhist teaching is to enable us to expand our consciousness by purifying our intention until we are able to awaken to this remarkable possibility.

Right Concentration – Meditation

The technique most associated with developing mindful awareness and purity of intention is the last of the eight steps on the Noble Path – Right Concentration or Meditation.

Most spiritual traditions stress the importance of self-reflection and prayer, but the Ganges civilisation at the time of the Buddha seems to have explored the practice of focused introspection in a more detailed, systematic and intensive way than any other, before or since.

We cannot be sure which precise meditation techniques the Buddha used or taught, but we do know from all the stories surrounding him that he spent a long time seated in silence, cultivating mindful awareness, and we also know that he constantly encouraged his followers to do the same.

The Buddha taught that there were four essential aspects to mindfulness: mindfulness of the body, mindfulness of feelings and emotions, mindfulness of mental processes and mindfulness of objects of thought. And he identified what he called Seven Factors of Awakening (*bodhyangas*): mindfulness, investigation of the mind, energy, joy, tranquillity, absorption and equanimity.

In essence, meditation helps us to observe our thought processes and reorientate ourselves psychologically. It calms, clarifies and balances our focus. It 'centres' us by loosening the tyranny of the attention-seeking mind. By bringing together concentration, intention and effort, meditation fosters awareness, composure and compassion.

The metaphor used most commonly is that of a pool of water.

> Too often the pool is agitated and muddy, reflecting nothing but its own turbidity. Buddhist meditation is designed to quieten the mind until it becomes perfectly still. Then the deep recesses of the pool can be seen clearly, and it will reflect a true picture of whatever is presented to it.[78]

The brain is a remarkably adaptive organ. There is now firm evidence that experienced meditators are able to modify its functioning – in effect, to reprogramme their minds and thus the way they experience and respond to internal and external stimuli. It is also possible to measure a range of specific health benefits: improved sleep, deeper relaxation, lower blood pressure and the slowing of age-related brain degeneration. The Dalai Lama has played an active role in supporting this 'mind and life' research, building a bridge with the scientific community as part of a broader discussion about the place of meditation in promoting wellbeing and happiness.[79]

Meditation takes many different forms – walking, chanting, prostrating and, in the Zen tradition, flower-arranging and tea-drinking. The form with which Buddhism is most commonly associated is seated meditation. Here again there are many variants but nearly all have these elements in common:

Posture – Adopting a physical position that is comfortable and unconstricted, a place in which to sit with a straight back and without being disturbed.

Breathing – Becoming aware of the breath. Steadying it. Breathing more deeply. Paying attention to its rise and fall.

Stilling – Becoming gradually quieter and calmer. Letting the concerns of the day fall away. Allowing the internal chatter to die down.

Focusing – Concentrating on the breath, on a focal point, mandala or image (if it is an open-eyed meditation) or on a sound (if it is a mantra).

Observing – Watching the busyness of the mind without judging or labelling it, as it seeks to distract and capture the attention.

Restoring – Gently bringing the focus back (the term 'escorting' is often used) each time it gets pulled away.

Going deeper – Practising and reinforcing this, until our minds get into the habit of being able to pay attention for extended periods of time and we feel confident that there is a secure and established inner space where we can rest, regroup and re-set our awareness.

Going outward again – Bringing Right Mind, Right Attention, and Right Intention into daily life until every aspect of what we do – the way we eat, drive, walk down the street, interact with our neighbours and work colleagues – becomes an aspect of meditation.

Obstacles

Much has been written about the various obstacles which arise in the course of meditation. They occur *inevitably* as part of the process, and practitioners are encouraged to see them not as problems but as opportunities for growth, in the same way that a surfer might seek out a bigger wave or a mountaineer might look for a steeper rock face to climb.

Some obstacles are very difficult to overcome – serious illness, bereavement or depression, for example – which can make meditating feel like the last thing one wants to do (though this is often when it is most beneficial). There are more subtle obstacles to practice in the form of distraction – busyness, intrusive requests, the mobile phone chirruping repeatedly. It is hard to practise if we have just eaten a big meal, or are angry or upset, or if friends are urging us to go out on the town with them. There is sleepiness, a feeling of overwhelming fatigue and sloth, which often assails us when there is something difficult at hand (revising for an exam, for example, or filling in a tax return).

Finally, there is that perennial obstacle: doubt – the persistent inner voice that tells us 'there's no point', 'it won't work,' 'it's a silly thing to do,' 'it's hopeless.' This is the voice we use to sabotage ourselves, so that we can triumphantly proclaim: 'You see: I told you I'd fail. I was right all along!'

The Buddha's battle with Mara epitomised his psychological confrontation with the forces of negativity and distraction. The world today is very different from the world of 450 BCE but the essence of the challenge remains the same: Can we sit calmly with ourselves? Can we still our minds? Can we see clearly into the reflective pool of our consciousness?

There is a great deal of information about meditation readily available on the internet, and many excellent resources on the topic. In terms of books it is hard to beat H. Saddhatissa's classic, *The Buddha's Way*, first published in 1971. In it he explores the two traditional types of meditation thought to date from the Buddha's time: Samatha, traditionally described as 'calming and concentrating' or serenity meditation, and Vipassana or 'insight' meditation which is more analytical and probing in its focus.[80]

The point of meditation is not, however, to confine one's practice to perfecting a particular technique, but, rather, to bring it into every aspect of daily life, at all times of day or night. In this regard meditation becomes a sensibility as much as a practice, something we do with every breath and step we take.

> The Buddha said to a novice, 'How long is the span of a man's life?' 'It is but a few days,' was the answer.
>
> The Buddha said, 'You have not understood,' and asked another man who said, 'It is like the time taken to eat a single meal.'
>
> To this the Buddha replied in the same way and asked a third: 'How long is the span of a man's life?'
>
> 'It is like a single breath,' was the reply.
>
> 'Excellent,' said the Buddha. 'You have understood the Way.'

The story above is cited by Vishvapani, a mindfulness teacher and Buddhist. He uses it as part of a reflection on the fundamental importance of breath:

Why is the span of life like a breath? A breath is very short and to describe life in this way emphasises its brevity. But there is more than that.

Breathing is an experience – a tangible, physical experience. It's with us all the time. All the time we are breathing in and breathing out in a continual cycle of inhalation and exhalation. We breathe in from the atmosphere and the body absorbs oxygen. We exhale the breath back into the world and we return carbon dioxide. Through the breath we are linked to the rest of life, we are bound up with the world.

And having breathed in, we must breathe out. Like death, it is natural and inevitable. If you pay attention to the breath you can feel directly within your own experience that we die each moment and that each moment we are reborn.

Understanding comes if we look deeply enough into simple things and dwell attentively on our actual experience.

So Breathe in. Breathe out. And pay attention.[81]

All meditation teachers throughout the ages would echo these words – and the Buddha himself would not have demurred.

Five Precepts

The Five Precepts are the nearest Buddhism comes to Christianity's Ten Commandments. There were several hundred rules for proper monastic conduct; but for lay adherents, not living under the particular conditions of a monastery, these are the five key undertakings:

1. Not to take life
2. Not to take what has not been given
3. Not to indulge in sexual misconduct
4. Not to speak falsely
5. Not to cloud the mind with intoxicants.

The Precepts appear emphatic in their negativity; but upon closer inspection they require a degree of wise interpretation. Rather than make dogmatic assertions, the Buddha preferred to set out a framework for consideration, then challenge people to work out the right behaviour according to circumstances and context.

The First Precept, for instance, does not say 'Thou shalt not kill' under any circumstances. Intention and motivation are, as ever, of prime importance. If we accidentally run over a cat in our hurry to take someone to hospital, our overriding motive is clear, even if our awareness is flawed.

So far so good. The same distinction is made in most legal codes between murder and manslaughter. But what about areas of extreme ethical complexity and controversy in the modern world: the debate around euthanasia, for example? Medical advances now make it possible to extend life – if 'life' is defined as brain or heart activity – via drugs and mechanical interventions. At what point does it become more compassionate to end physical existence than to allow it to continue? It is impossible, surely, to be universally prescriptive on such topics? Decisions must come down to the specifics of any given case.

Similarly, the Buddha's pragmatic advice on vege-tarianism was that mendicants should graciously accept whatever was offered to them in their begging bowls – including meat – provided animals had not been killed specifically in order to feed them. He was emphatic in his stress on the preciousness of life for all sentient beings, but practical wisdom must be applied to the precise circumstances of each case.

A similar care with interpretation relates to the Second Precept. 'Not to take what has not been given' is not the same as not stealing. We might find a purse on the pavement, for instance. We have not stolen it but neither does it belong to us.

Once this concept of rightful ownership is extended, where does it lead? What does it mean to 'take what has not been given' when it comes to natural resources, for example? If an individual can own the oil beneath the ground, why not the air above it? The Buddha had no personal possessions other than his robe of stitched-together rags, a razor, a water strainer and his mendicant's bowl. In this he felt himself liberated rather than deprived. But he was well aware that his chosen way of life was not suitable for everyone.

The Third Precept, refraining from 'sexual misconduct' is not as specific an injunction as 'Thou shalt not commit adultery' or 'Thou shalt not covet thy neighbour's husband or wife.' In contrast to Roman Catholic orthodoxy, for example, the Third Precept neither proscribes nor prescribes certain sexual practices on certain days under certain conditions. The Buddha himself was a renunciant (having previously been married and a father) so we must presume that he thought celibacy conducive to his own awakening, but not all Buddhists believe that monasticism and chastity are necessary pre-requisites for enlightenment.

The Fourth Precept is 'not to speak falsely'. Again, this is not the same as not lying. Half-truths can be more deceptive than outright falsehoods. When we speak, is our desire to encourage and uplift the person we are speaking to? Are we trying to understand them, or are we trying to show how clever we are? Is what we say authentic, sincere, compassionate, helpful? Are the words we deploy likely to achieve a wise and beneficial outcome?

> Giving up false speech he becomes a speaker of truth, reliable, trustworthy, dependable, he does not deceive the world. Giving up malicious speech he does not repeat there what he has heard here nor does he repeat here what he has heard there in order to cause variance between people. He reconciles those who are divided and brings closer together those who are already friends. Harmony is his joy, harmony is his delight, harmony is his love; it is the motive of his speech. Giving up harsh speech, his speech is blameless, pleasing to the ear, agreeable, going to the heart, urbane, liked by most. Giving up idle chatter he speaks at the right time, what is correct, to the point ... He speaks words worth being treasured, seasonable, reasonable, well defined and to the point.[82]

There is some debate about whether the Fifth Precept prohibits all potential intoxicants or, rather, permits their responsible use provided they do not have an intoxicating effect! The lines of the discussion are finely drawn. What is beyond dispute is that alcohol and substance abuse are serious problems in the modern world. Addiction, it seems, is something our society struggles to approach in a mature and consistent way. Certain drugs are prohibited, while others, whose effects may be more pernicious, are permitted and even promoted. One of the key aims of Buddhist practice is to sharpen awareness and clarify the workings of the mind, so it behoves us to be very wary of substances which cloud or in any way disrupt our consciousness.

Death

Perhaps the Buddha's best-known teaching was his last. To compress forty-five years into a few brief pages and fast-forward to the end of such a long and rich life is to miss out much historical detail and colour. Not explored in this book, for example, are a series of dramatic powerplays as the two great warlords, King Bimbisara of Magadha and King Prasenajit of Kosala, battled with each other, only to be usurped and murdered at the behest of their sons.[83] Meanwhile, despite the Buddha's earnest pleas for tolerance, his Shakya clan was all but annihilated and its lands annexed. Far from living happily ever after, with all the peoples of the region co-existing in harmony, the rivalries between them intensified.

The Buddha's latter years were times of widespread suffering and anxiety.

In terms of the contours of the legend, however, the Buddha's death not only marks the conclusion of his life story; it also points to the heart of his message.

As we have seen, death – or, rather, what happens to us after we die – was a topic the Buddha was loath to discuss.[84] Asked where people go when they die, he turned the question back on the questioner: 'Where does a flame go when it is blown out?' It doesn't 'go' anywhere: it is simply that the process of combustion ceases.

The ending of samsara is what is known as nirvana. One translation is 'quenching' or 'blowing out', in the way that a thirst is slaked or the flame of a candle is snuffed. In the course of his teachings, the Buddha used many different ways to describe this state:

'harbour of refuge', 'cool cave', 'island amidst the floods', 'place of bliss', 'emancipation', 'liberation', 'safety', 'the transcendental', 'the uncreated', 'the tranquil', 'the home of ease', 'the calm', 'the end of suffering', 'the medicine for all evil', 'the unshaken', 'ambrosia', 'the immaterial', 'the imperishable', 'the abiding', 'the further shore', 'the unending', 'the bliss of effort', 'the supreme joy', 'the ineffable', 'detachment'. [85]

As to 'final nirvana' (*parinirvana*) which, according to one famous sutra, the Buddha was supposed to attain when he died and from which he would never be reborn in human form, where did he 'go' then? The texts talk of a state of being which can only be described in terms an absence – 'deathless, unaging, unailing, sorrowless, undefiled',[86] 'unborn, unoriginated, uncreated and unformed'.

There is that dimension where there is neither earth, nor water, nor fire, nor wind; neither dimension of the infinitude of space, nor dimension of the infinitude of consciousness, nor dimension of nothingness, nor dimension of neither perception nor non-perception; neither this world, nor the next world, nor sun, nor moon. And there, I say, there is neither coming, nor going, nor stasis; neither passing away nor arising: without stance, without foundation, without support.[87]

The Buddha approached his final days calmly and in good cheer. The precise cause of his death is unclear. It seems to have been related to an attack of dysentery brought on by a contaminated meal, but he was already very long-lived by this time and getting increasingly frail.

I am now grown old, Ananda, and full of years; my journey is done and I have reached the sum of my days; I am turning eighty years of age. And just as a worn out cart is kept going with the help of repairs, so it seems is (my) body kept going with repairs ... Do not sorrow. Do not lament. Have I not explained that it is the nature of things that we must be divided and parted from all that is beloved and dear?[88]

Slowly he made his way back towards his family home in Kapilavastu. At a place called Kushinagara, he selected a grove of sal trees and lay down under their shade. His followers gathered round him, knowing that the end was near. The texts relate how he carried on encouraging them right up to the last minute. Indeed, he took the opportunity to make his final teaching the most urgent and pithy of all, the distillation of his lifetime's experience:

Nothing lasts for ever. Strive hard to work out your enlightenment.[89]

Then he reclined on his right side, resting his head on his hand (the pose in which so many statues show him.) The legend tells how the birds stopped singing, the breezes stilled, and thick blossom from the surrounding trees began to fall onto his body as he lay there and breathed his last.

3

Afterlife: Buddhism after the Buddha

THE FINAL SECTION of this book brings the story of the Buddha up to date and looks at how his teachings live on in the world today. It traces Buddhism's growth, transmission and development into a global movement, a worldwide community of lay and monastic adherents.

This community, or Sangha as it is known, is the third of what Buddhists refer to as the three 'jewels', 'treasures, or 'refuges' – together with the teaching (Dharma) and the person (Buddha). In the view of Thich Nhat Hanh, 'It is difficult if not impossible to practise the way of understanding and love without a sangha, a community of friends who practise the same way,' and there is no doubt that without the commitment of countless devoted supporters across the generations the Buddha's words would be lost to us today.[90]

Innumerable sanghas have passed in and out of existence since the Buddha's death, each shaped by a different history, geography and culture. But they all trace their origins back to the moment when the Buddha preached his first sermon in the deer park in Isipatana and set in motion what texts call the 'Wheel of the Dharma', ushering in a new era in the history of human consciousness. [91]

Word of his teaching spread quickly. Shramanas came from far away to hear this new sage from Shakya. A group soon formed around him. These were literally fellow travellers, for wherever he went on his journey they went too, walking with him along the banks of the River Ganges, sharing food, asking questions and exploring his teachings. When the heavy monsoon rains made travel difficult – the wet season typically lasts four months – they would gather together in simple accommodation on parkland at the outskirts of the bigger towns.

Over the years these centres (known as *vihara* – 'a secluded place in which to walk') became semi-permanent, and ultimately they evolved into autonomous, self-governing monasteries where monks could take up full-time residence. It was an arrangement with advantages for everyone. The monks could devote more time to meditation, while for the lay community the monastery provided much-needed medical and educational support and a focal point for religious practice.

The most famous of these retreat sites was Jetavana ('Jeta's grove') in the state of Kosala. It had been purchased at enormous expense by a local merchant called Anathapindika, who then donated it for use by the sangha. The Buddha spent some nineteen rainy seasons there over the course of his teaching mission.

The names of some of the Buddha's sangha have come down to us through history. The two monks most highly regarded for their intellectual and mental prowess were called Maudgalyayana and Shariputra. Also mentioned frequently in the texts is the Buddha's cousin and devoted personal assistant, Ananda. Devadatta, his cousin, was a more controversial presence who later vied for control of the sangha and may even have conspired to get the Buddha killed.[92]

Other clan members who joined the sangha – for the Buddha was eventually reconciled with his family – included his son Rahula, his half-brother Nanda, and his stepmother/aunt, Prajapati. History records her as the first woman to follow the renunciant path and affiliate herself as a nun. The Buddha's agreement to allow women into the sangha was a radical and controversial decision at the time, and is still to this day regarded as problematic by some of Asia's more patriarchal communities. With hindsight it seems remarkably visionary.[93]

Recollection

Shortly after the Buddha had passed away, his followers were summoned by a senior monk, Mahakashyapa, to a council near the local capital, Rajagriha. At this meeting a record of the Buddha's teachings was compiled, based on recollections of what he had said during the course of his long life. Particularly important in this process were the contributions of two members of the sangha: Upali, who concentrated on the Buddha's teachings about proper monastic conduct; and Ananda, the Buddha's cousin and confidant who had spent twenty-five years in close attendance. Ananda had a prodigious memory and it is said that he was able to recite by heart all the teachings he had heard over the course of his lifetime's devotion.

A consensus was reached. Through repeated recitation the teachings were memorised collectively to be passed on from generation to generation. Over time – though not until some four centuries later – the teachings were eventually written down. A literary canon (streamlined, standardised and more than likely simplified) began to emerge, a vast body of work running to many thousands of pages. The later Chinese and Tibetan canons are even more voluminous.

There has been continuous scholarly investigation into which elements are 'authentic' and which were added by commentators and teachers other than the Buddha. It is an endless source of debate and enrichment – as well as potential dispute and discord.

> Now, monks, I say to you that these teachings of which I have direct knowledge and which I have made known to you – these you should thoroughly learn, cultivate, develop, and frequently practice, that the life of purity may be established and may long endure, for the welfare and happiness of the multitude, out of compassion for the world, for the benefit, well being, and happiness of gods and men.
>
> And what, monks, are these teachings? They are the four foundations of mindfulness, the four right efforts, the four constituents of psychic power, the five faculties, the five powers, the seven factors of enlightenment, and the Noble Eightfold Path.[94]

Ashoka – and After

The decisive moment in Buddhism's transformation from a local into a world religion occurred about 150 years after the Buddha's death. The dominant regional power of the age was the Mauryan Empire, and the dominant personality was its emperor, Ashoka, who ruled from c.273–232 BCE. Legend has it that he was sickened by the carnage of one particularly gruesome battle and became an overnight convert to the Buddha's teachings.

A man of exceptional vision and energy, Ashoka began to promote peace as vigorously as he had previously prosecuted war. He decreed that Buddhist inscriptions be carved at various staging posts around his empire. He endowed monasteries and hospitals. He despatched emissaries (including his own son Mahendra and daughter Sanghamitra) to spread the teachings overseas. His endorsement of Buddhism, like the Roman Emperor Constantine's support for Christianity five hundred or so years later, was instrumental in turning it from a regional into a global phenomenon.

South of the Subcontinent, Buddhism reached Sri Lanka where it quickly took root and flourished. From there it travelled across the seas to South-East Asia – modern-day Thailand, Burma, Laos and Cambodia.

North and east of the Himalayas it diffused along the silk route into China and then on to Korea, Vietnam and Japan.

The great adventurer Marco Polo (1254–1324) was fascinated to encounter Buddhists on his travels in Asia. Many were merchant travellers who seemed able to mingle comfortably with people from different cultures. There is even a suggestion that the teachings reached Classical Europe – though no tangible evidence for this has emerged as yet.

Going Global

The next key phase in the transmission of Buddhism came with the revolution in transport and communications towards the second half of the nineteenth century. Ocean-going ships, steam-powered railways and improved mapping brought about the beginnings of mass migration. Intrepid explorers, imperial adventurers, missionaries and scholars from Europe and America came face to face with exotic Oriental cultures. More significantly, the indigenous poor from these Asiatic countries were able to emigrate to the West in search of a better life.

Initially these migrant communities stayed separate and self-contained, while, among the host population, the study and practice of Buddhism remained very much a minority academic interest. Then, in the 1960s, a new, 'hippy' culture began to emerge. For a time, among the younger generation at least, it became fashionable to be interested in esoteric Eastern religions. The Beatles grew beards and adopted a guru (albeit not a Buddhist one). A New Age was born.

The last half-century has witnessed a dramatic growth in the awareness of Buddhism and of the Buddha's teachings in the West. There are posters promoting the benefits of meditation in health centres up and down the land. Mindfulness classes are taught in hundreds of schools, colleges and therapy groups. Books by Thich Nhat Hanh, Jack Kornfield, Joseph Goldstein, Sharon Salzberg, Pema Chödrön and others have sold in their tens of thousands. And the face of the Dalai Lama has become one of the best known in the world.

Diversity

One of the features of this remarkable 2,500-year journey of transmission is Buddhism's great diversity of expression. The Buddha consistently refused to anoint a successor to lead the fellowship of monks after he died. Instead he emphasised the importance of consensus, communal harmony and personal responsibility, urging the monks to focus on the Dharma and become 'islands of refuge' unto themselves.

This means there is no Buddhist equivalent to a pope or grand imam – no single authority figure. Buddhism is certainly not immune to authoritarian impulses or abuses, especially where the teacher is accorded undue veneration, but the Buddha's opposition to hierarchy makes it doctrinally impossible to come up with a notion like that of papal infallibility or divine revelation.

Moreover, because the Buddha's teachings were delivered in person, in conversations and discourses tailored to the specific questions and needs of his audience, and because they were spoken rather than written down, there is no overriding or 'definitive' statement or credo such as might have emerged in a written culture. The teachings were made at different times, to different people at different levels of awareness. This made them more pertinent at the time; and it also renders them more open to ongoing reinterpretation in light of changing circumstances.

For some observers the resulting 'plurality of narratives' is confusing. For others Buddhism's flexibility and freedom from dogma is the very reason it has been able to adapt so well and remain modern and relevant in an increasingly diverse world.

Signs of this diversity were visible from the outset. At the First Council of Rajagriha the sangha was relatively unified and able to agree about the Buddha's most important teachings. But by the time of the Second Council, held at Vaisali a century or so later, and the Third (Pataliputra) Council approximately 150 years after the Buddha's death, this consensus had started to evaporate. In particular, different interpretations of the vinaya teachings regulating monastic life had begun to emerge – fuelled no doubt by personal rivalries as well as broader cultural and theological differences.

As the teachings of Buddhism spread and the institutions supporting them multiplied, so the differences both between and within different traditions proliferated and became ever more accentuated, as if propelled by a giant centrifuge. A Zen monastery in Japan (austere, silent) and a Kagyu monastery in Tibet (colourful, noisy) are, on the face of it, worlds apart. But then so are their host cultures. Buddhist monks wear different coloured robes (maroon in Tibet, saffron in Sri Lanka, grey in Japan) and recite different liturgies. Some commentators have suggested that we should talk not of Buddhism but of Buddhisms in the plural, for the singular noun conveys a misleading sense of unity and coherence. Others point out that there are differences within all religious traditions. Unlike the Protestant/Roman Catholic schism in Christianity or the Shia/Sunni conflict in Islam, Buddhists do not have a history of large-scale sectarian killing – although internecine rivalry is not unknown and recent atrocities in Sri Lanka, Thailand and Burma make it clear that killing and intimidation can occur in Buddhist cultures too, despite the Buddha's categorical and emphatic teaching about non-violence (*ahimsa*).

In Britain there are over a thousand Buddhist groups to explore. The Network of Buddhist Organisations (NBO), established in 1993, is the best port of call for information: www.nbo.org.uk. Nearly three thousand groups (the actual figure is much higher) are listed on www.Buddhanet.org for North America. They range from the Accidental Buddhist Sangha to the ZenwordsZencentre, which gives some idea of the spectrum of possibilities. As the note on the NBO homepage puts it:

For those non-Buddhists who visit this site seeking information about Buddhism, we would remind you that there are many diverse traditions and schools of Buddhism. Interpretations of teachings may differ from school to school, so care should be taken in drawing any conclusion as to the generality of any specific interpretation. You should also know that there are growing numbers of reputable secular groups that teach mindfulness.[95]

Not all Buddhists are vegetarians, or agree about the role of women in society, or the best way to prevent war. Not all meditate cross-legged, or concur about what it means to be enlightened. But the fact people consciously assume the label 'Buddhist' suggests that there must be some sense of shared beliefs, approaches and attitudes. And the one thing they *all* have in common is gratitude for the person and teachings of the Buddha.

Living Buddha

And so we come back once again to the figure of Siddhartha Gautama, the source of it all, the 'fountain-head ... for all the evolving streams of ... doctrine and practice throughout the centuries'.[96] How is it that a penniless wanderer dressed in rags, walking the dusty roads of an ancient civilisation, in a world without reading and writing – let alone mobile phones and personal computers – still speaks to us with power and relevance twenty-five centuries later?

The answer lies in the fact that the Buddha was able to see so far beyond the material conditions of his own particular age.[97] His vision was extraordinary. He understood the human condition, human experience and the basis of human suffering, with a clarity and depth that remains unsurpassed. His analysis of change, contingency and transience is strikingly in tune with modern life. So too his exploration of psychology, with his emphasis on motivation, subjectivity and the plasticity of consciousness. His prescription of mindful awareness, ethics training and self-transformation is as apt now as it was all those lifetimes ago. Moreover, in his analysis of interdependence he highlighted perhaps the most important concept with which to approach the challenges of the twenty-first century. His is a message that transcends national, regional, ethnic, racial, cultural (and indeed religious) differences.

Regimes come and go. Empires rise and fall. Orthodoxies become heresies. But the existential challenge at an individual level remains the same today as it did in the age of the Buddha. Greed, hatred and ignorance still lie at the root of suffering. Wisdom, courage and compassion are still at the heart of what makes the world a better place. In the words of the Dalai Lama, 'the Buddha's essential message of compassion, ethical responsibility, mental tranquility, and discernment is as relevant today as it was more than 2,500 years ago ... Put[ting] it into practice ... is essential for the creation of a happier and more peaceful world.'⁹⁸

Are we on the Eightfold Path or not? Are we even looking for a path? Are we striving hard to work out our enlightenment? Are we fostering a 'culture of awakening' or one of delusion? The questions the Buddha posed on his travels remain as incisive now as they did in his own time. And they are getting ever more urgent.

In order to transform the poisons into medicine every society and every individual must cultivate the necessary skills anew. This involves time, effort and patience. It is a lifetime project. No one, not even the Buddha, can do it for us.

Start

'It is rare to be born a human being. The number of those endowed with human life is as small as the amount of earth one can place on a fingernail.'⁹⁹ And life is short.

Just as a dewdrop on the tip of a blade of grass ... the life of human beings is brief and fleeting ... like a bubble on the surface of the water, the life of human beings is brief and fleeting ... like a line drawn on water ... You should heed advice, do what is wholesome, practise the spiritual life; there is no escape from death for one who is born.[100]

This is the essence of the Buddha's teaching. Nothing lasts forever. Strive hard to work out your enlightenment. Breathe deep. Be happy. And help others to become happy too. Start here. Start now.

Wake up!

Notes

1   'Number of Buddhists World-Wide', Buddhanet.net, 2008,
    www.buddhanet.net/e-learning/history/bud_statwrld.
    htm. Some scholars argue that: (1) Buddhism is not really a
    religion, since it is non-theistic (2) Buddhism takes so many
    variant forms that the singular term 'Buddhism' is misleading.
    All of which has made the writing of even this modest volume
    extremely challenging!
2   https://en.wikipedia.org/wiki/Buddhism_by_country
3   Goodman, Sandra, 'Review of Dalai Lama, *An Open Heart –
    Practising Compassion in Everyday Life*', Positive Health Online,
    www.positivehealth.com/review/an-open-heart-practising-
    compassion-in-everyday-life
4   Mitchell, Margaret, 'Thich Nhat Hanh and Martin Luther
    King', Charter for Compassion, 2015, www.charterforcompas-
    sion.org/index.php/practicing-peace/thich-nhat-hanh-and-
    martin-luther-king
5   Thich Vinh Minh, 'Aung San Suu Kyi with Q–A on
    Buddhism', YouTube, 18 August 2013, www.youtube.com/
    watch?v=amHroRGdq0E
6   Silberman, Steve, 'What Kind of Buddhist Was Steve Jobs,
    Really?' PLoS Blogs, 26 October 2015, http://blogs.plos.org/
    neurotribes/2015/10/26/what-kind-of-buddhist-was-steve-
    jobs-really
7   'Postscript: Many Names for the Buddha,' in 'A Sketch of
    the Buddha's Life: Readings from the Pali Canon,' Access to
    Insight, 30 November 2013, www.accesstoinsight.org/ptf/
    buddha.html#ps
8   There is debate about whether or not this name was an inven-
    tion by subsequent devotees.

9   For maps of where Buddha lived and taught, Google: "images for map of India in the time of the Buddha" and "images for maps of Buddhism spread".

10 Armstrong, Karen, *Buddha* (Phoenix, 2002) pp.16–17.

11 Gombrich, Richard, 'Dating the Buddha: a Red Herring Revealed', in *The Dating of the Historical Buddha Part 2 (Symposien zur Buddhismusforschung, IV, 2)*, (Vandenhoeck & Ruprecht, 1992) pp.237–259.

12 Armstrong, Karen, *Buddha*, p.xvii; Batchelor, Stephen, *Confessions of a Buddhist Atheist* (Spiegel & Grau, 2011), p.101; Lamotte, cited in Gethin, Rupert, *The Foundations of Buddhism* (OPUS, 1998), pp.12–13; Gombrich, Richard, *What the Buddha Thought* (Equinox, 2009) p.17.

13 The image on the cover of this book is named 'Golden Buddha' and comes from sixteenth-century Thailand © iStockphoto.

14 Carrithers, Michael, *The Buddha* (OUP, 2001) p.8.

15 See the many writings of the great mythologist Joseph Campbell, summarised at Montrean, Fred, 'Jospeh Campbell's Hero's Journey Abridged', YouTube, 5 May 2013, www.youtube.com/watch?v=kJwPIiUPfK4

16 See Epstein, Mark, *The Trauma of Everyday Life* (Hay House, 2014).

17 Vishvapani Blomfield, *Gautama Buddha: The Life and Teachings of the Awakened One* (Quercus, 2011) p.23.

18 Armstrong, *Buddha*, p.29.

19 This translation of the story (including the quotations which follow) is from Jinananda, *Warrior of Peace: The Life of the Buddha* (Windhorse, 2002) pp. 21–22.

20 Gethin, Rupert, *Sayings of the Buddha: New Translations from the Pali Nikayas* (World's Classics, 2008) p.19.

21 For a useful summary of these states or meditative planes see Carrithers, *The Buddha,* pp.31–37. On yoga see Armstrong, *Buddha*, pp.43–57.

22 For a British equivalent see: Morris, Tony, 'Cuthbert', Anglo-Saxon Portraits, BBC Radio 3 on iPlayer, 25 October 2012,

www.bbc.co.uk/iplayer/episode/b01ngr4k/The_Essay_For
Saxon_Portraits_Cuthbert

23 Jinananda's translation of the *Majjhima Nikaya* 36.26–28 in
Warrior of Peace, p.40.

24 *Samyutta Nikaya* 56.11 www.accesstoinsight.org/tipitaka/sn/
sn56/sn56.011.than.html

25 Armstrong, *Buddha,* p.64.

26 Jinananda, *Warrior of Peace*, p.46 (translation of Asvaghosa,
Buddhacarita 12.120).

27 See Batchelor, Stephen, *Living With The Devil: A Meditation on
Good and Evil* (Riverhead, 2005).

28 Cited in Hope, Jane and van Loon, Borin, *Introducing Buddha*
(Icon, 2008) p.20.

29 Nanamoli and Bodhi, *A Translation of the Majjhima Nikaya*
(Wisdom, 3rd edition) p.1015.

30 Jayawickrama, N.A. (trans.) *Jataka Nidana: The Story of Gotama
Buddha* (Pali Text Society, 1990) p.99.

31 Prebish, Charles S. and Keown, Damien, *Buddhism: The eBook.
An Online Introduction* (4th edition) p.10.

32 The literature on this topic is extensive – and much contested.
See, for example, Gombrich, *What the Buddha Thought*,
pp.26–28 on what he calls 'the problem of theodicy'.

33 Batchelor, Stephen, 'Rebirth: A Case for Buddhist Agnosticism',
Martine and Stephen Batchelor website, www.stephenbatch-
elor.org/index.php/en/rebirth-a-case-for-buddhist-agnosticism

34 My colloquial rendition. For the full exchange as set out in
the *Majjgima Nikaya 63* see www.accesstoinsight.org/tipitaka/
mn/mn.063.than.html

35 *Majjhima Nikaya 36.* See 'Awakening' in 'A Sketch of the
Buddha's Life: Readings from the Pali Canon', Access to
Insight, 30 November 2013, www.accesstoinsight.org/ptf/
buddha.html#awakening

36 Bhikkhu Bodhi, *The Connected Discourses of the Buddha: A
Translation of the Samyutta Nikaya* (Wisdom, 2000) p.552.

37 *Dhammapada* verse, cited in http://online.sfsu.edu/rone/
Buddhism/footsteps.htm

38 Vishvapani, *Gautama Buddha*, p.152.

39 Traditional proverb – origin unknown.

40 *Jataka Nidana – The Story of Gotama Buddha,* p.99.

41 For a description of how the teaching about the chain of twelve nidanas developed, see Gombrich, *What the Buddha Thought*, pp.129ff. On what is called in Japanese *ichinen sanzen*, see www.sgi.org/about-us/buddhism-in-daily-life/three-thousand-realms-in-a-single-moment-of-life.html

42 The term 'Interbeing' is most often associated with Thich Nhat Hanh. In Chapter 18 of his *Old Path, White Clouds: The Life Story of the Buddha* he attempts to convey his sense of the Buddha's realisation.

43 Ikeda, Daisaku, *The Living Buddha: An Interpretive Biography* (Middleway, 2008) p.68. This is very much a Mahayana emphasis. Elsewhere Ikeda writes: 'The cosmos is not so big that life cannot embrace it nor a particle of matter so small that life cannot be contained within it.' www.facebook.com/permalink.php?id=453800101347901&story_fbid=591513394243237

44 This is, of course, imagined – but it chimes with most experiences of epiphany. See Irvine, William B., *Aha! The Moments of Insight that Shape our World* (OUP, 2015).

45 In the legend the god Brahma appears to him and pleas with Buddha to share his understanding with the world.

46 Gethin, *Sayings of the Buddha*, p.62.

47 Verses from the *Dhammapada*: 103 and 222.

48 Soma Thera (trans.) 'Kalama Sutta: The Instruction to the Kalamas', Access to Insight, 30 November 2013, www.accessto-insight.org/tipitaka/an/an03/an03.065.soma.html

49 *Majjhima Nikaya* 1.265, quoted in Carrithers, *The Buddha*, p.4.

50 This story does not appear in the Pali texts. It is first recorded in 1036 CE. This does not mean that it didn't occur – but it does highlight the difficulty ascertaining what the historic Buddha taught and what others said he taught.

51 Gombrich, *What the Buddha Thought,* p.ix.

52 Later elaborated by the scholar Nagarjuna (c.150–250 CE) into the doctrine known as *Sunyata* or 'emptiness' – i.e.

phenomena are void of essence or intrinsic existence: there is no reality or non-reality, only relativity.

53 See Morris, Tony, *Buddhism by Numbers* (Mud Pie, 2019).

54 I use the Pali term here as it is more commonly used than the Sanskrit 'Duhkha'. See the many variant interpretations at https://en.wikipedia.org/wiki/Dukkha.

55 Carrithers, *The Buddha*, p.57.

56 The evidence suggests that stress and anxiety levels in the so-called 'developed world' have never been higher. See Osterman, Cynthia (ed.), 'More than One in Ten Americans Use Antidepressants', Reuters, 19 October 2011, www.reuters.com/article/2011/10/19/us-usa-antidepressants-idUSTRE79I7FI20111019

57 *Samyutta Nikaya* 56, www.accesstoinsight.org/ptf/dhamma/sacca/sacca1/

58 See, inter alia, Offer, Avner, *The Challenge of Affluence: Self-Control and Well-Being in the United States and Britain since 1950* (OUP, 2006).

59 Stephen Batchelor's translation, *Confession*, p.253.

60 *Anguttara Nikaya* 2, Bikkhu Bodhi, *In the Buddha's Words*, p.35.

61 *Samyutta Nikaya* 22, www.accesstoinsight.org/tipitaka/sn/sn22/sn22.059.than.html

62 'Changing Poison into Medicine', Soka Gakkai International, 2015, www.sgi.org/about-us/buddhism-in-daily-life/changing-poison-into-medicine.html

63 Armstrong, *Buddha,* p.104.

64 Conradi, Peter J., *Going Buddhist: Panic and Emptiness, the Buddha and Me* (Short Books, 2005).

65 This is Thich Nhat Hanh imagining the words of the Buddha in *Old Path, White Clouds,* p.175.

66 There is insufficient space here to explore or even adequately outline the various and remarkably sophisticated Buddhist analyses of consciousness – material form, feelings, perception, volition, mental formations and sensory consciousness – let alone their complex interrelationship. A good starting point is to look up '*Skandhas*' in Gombrich, *What the Buddha Taught.*

67 *Samyutta Nikaya* 22.99, in Bikkhu Bodhi, *In the Buddha's Words,*
     p.40.
68 Ikeda, Daisaku, 'The Jewel Hidden in the Robe', Soka Gakkai
     International, 2015, www.sgi.org/about-us/president-ikedas-
     writings/the-jewel-hidden-in-the-robe.html
69 'Stephen Batchelor on the Four Noble Tasks', Upaya
     Zen Center, 2 February 2015, www.upaya.org/2015/02/
     stephen-batchelor-four-noble-tasks
70 *Sumyatta Nikaya* 4.35, in Vishvapani, *Gautama Buddha*, p.127.
     For a brilliant analysis of the role of fire in the teaching of the
     Buddha see Gombrich, *What the Buddha Thought*, chapter 8.
71 Gethin, *Sayings of the Buddha,* p.45.
72 Verses from the *Dhammapada* quoted in Harris, Elizabeth J.
     and Kauth, Ramona (eds), *Meeting Buddhists* (Christians Aware,
     2004) pp.288–30.
73 Harris, Elizabeth J., *What Buddhists Believe* (Oneworld, 1998)
     p.38.
74 Gombrich, *What the Buddha Thought,* p.127. See chapters 8 and
     9. See also Gombrich, Richard, *How Buddhism Began* (Routledge,
     2nd edition, 2011) p.51.
75 Armstrong, *Buddha*, p.100.
76 HH Dalai Lama and Cutler, Howard, *The Art of Happiness: A
     Handbook for Living* (Hodder, 1999) p.2.
77 A deceptively simple statement! Some schools think the
     process takes many lifetimes, others that it is available to all
     of us in this lifetime.
78 Saddhatissa, H., *The Buddha's Way* (George Braziller, 1972) p.57.
79 www.dailycardinal.com/news/2005/02/01/Science/Meditation.
     Provides.longTerm.Benefits-847382.shtml and www.meaningfo-
     life.i12.com/meditation-article.htm. Links to the Mind and Life
     Institute can be found at: www.mindandlife.org
80 Pali terms are used here as they are better known than the
     Sanskrit *Shamatha* and *Vipasyana*.
81 Vishvapani, 'Breathe in ... and See Impermanence', Wise
     Attention, 21 December 2011, www.wiseattention.org/
     blog/2011/12/21/breathe-in-and-see-impermanence

82 *Majjhima Nikaya* 1.179, in Dhammasaavaka, *The Buddhist Primer* (2005) p.41. Thich Nhat Hanh is wonderful on the subject of talking – and listening: see *The Art of Communicating* (Rider Books, 2013) pp.37–90.

83 The sons' names were Ajatashatru and Virudhaka. Their stories make tragic and blood-curdling reading.

84 See above note 34.

85 A list compiled by Vishvapani in *Gautama Buddha*, p.94.

86 *Majjhima Nikaya* 26, in Bhikkhu Bodhi, *In the Buddha's Words*, p.59.

87 *Udana* 8.1 and 8.3, www.accesstoinsight.org/tipitaka/kn/ud/ud.8.01.than.html

88 Quoted in Gethin, *Foundations of Buddhism*, p.26.

89 There are many variants on this. See Morris, Tony, *What Do Buddhists Believe?* n.15, p.84.

90 Thich Nhat Hanh, *Teachings on Love* (Parallax Press, 2007) p.132.

91 Interestingly the wheel features at the centre of the current Indian flag even though India is now a predominantly Hindu country.

92 Vishvapani's theory about Devadatta is more plausible to my mind: see Vishvapani, *Gautama Buddha*, pp.258–60.

93 Despite the Buddha's fundamentally humanistic, inclusive and egalitarian teachings, sexism, mysogyny and patriarchy have featured in many of its institutions.

94 *Digha Nikaya* 16.

95 www.nbo.org.uk

96 Bhikku Bodhi, *In the Buddha's Words*, p.ix.

97 See Batchelor, *Confession*, pp.237–38.

98 Dalia Lama, Foreword to Bikkhu Bodhi, *In the Buddha's Words*, pp.vii–viii.

99 *Writings of Nichiren Daishonin*, vol 1: 106: www.nichirenlibrary.org/en/wnd-1/Content/106#para-16.

100 Araka (A IV 137-8) quoted in Gethin, *Sayings of the Buddha*, pp.261–62.

Further Reading

Armstrong, Karen, *Buddha: His Life and Thought* (Weidenfeld & Nicolson, 2000).

Batchelor, Stephen, *Buddhism without Beliefs* (Bloomsbury, 1998).

Batchelor, Stephen, *Confession of a Buddhist Atheist* (Spiegel & Grau, 2011).

Bhikkhu Bodhi, *In the Buddha's Words* (Wisdom, 2005).

Carrithers, Michael, *The Buddha* (OUP, 1983).

Conradi, Peter J., *Going Buddhist* (Short Books, 2006).

Gethin, Rupert, *The Foundations of Buddhism* (OUP, 1998).

Gethin, Rupert, *Sayings of the Buddha* (OUP, 2008).

Gombrich, Richard, *How Buddhism Began* (Routledge, 2011).

Gombrich, Richard, *What the Buddha Thought* (Equinox, 200).

Hesse, Hermann, *Siddhartha* (Penguin Classics, 2002).

Ikeda, Daisaku, *The Living Buddha* (Weatherhill, 1998).

Jinananda, *Warrior of Peace* (Windhorse, 2002).

Keown, Damien, *Buddhist Ethics: A Very Short Introduction* (OUP, 2005).

Morris, Tony, *What Do Buddhists Believe?* (Granta, 2005).

Morris, Tony, *Buddhism by Numbers* (Mud Pie, 2019).

Saddhatissa, H., *The Life of the Buddha* (Allen & Unwin, 1976).

Thich Nhat Hanh, *Old Path, White Clouds* (Rider, 1991).

Vishvapani, *Gautama Buddha* (Quercus, 2011).

Walpola, Rahula, *What the Buddha Taught* (Oneworld, 1997).

Web Links

A Google search for 'Buddhism' returns over 200 million hits! All the main schools have web pages and there are numerous academic and personal sites, most of which contain further links. Here are some of the places I've found most useful:

www.accesstoinsight.org – Readings in Theravada Buddhism, and much else besides.

www.buddhanet.net – An exceptionally comprehensive resource featuring all sorts of sections, including further weblinks, a recommended list of the Top Ten Buddhist Websites: www.buddhanet.net/10_best. htm and a World Buddhist Directory: www. buddhanet.info/wbd

www.dharmanet.org – An extensive list of groups, publications and study materials, including 'Socially Engaged Buddhism Resources'.

Guides to Buddhist centres and information about retreat centres and events are readily available online. A simple Google search will do the trick.

There are various Buddhist newsletters, magazines and audio resources:

   www.audiodharma.org – A wonderful podcast resource.

   www.dharmaseed.org – Another great podcast library.

   www.lionsroar.com – Curated content from *Shambhala Sun* and *Buddhadharma*.

   www.tricycle.com/magazine – The best-known Buddhist magazine.

There are also some very helpful Twitter lists. Why not start here and follow the comment thread:

www.lionsroar.com/
      studying-buddhism-online-where-to-go/

Finally, two of my personal favourites:

   www.ocbs.org – The Oxford Centre for Buddhist Studies.

   www.appliedbuddhism.org.uk/library-institute-oriental-philosophy – The Library of the Institute for Oriental Philosophy at the Centre for Applied Buddhism.

Acknowledgements

I began writing this book half a lifetime ago. It has become much, much harder as time has gone on – a genuine case of the more you find out the less you know. Friends and scholars have offered advice, support and comment along the way: Nick Allen, Chris Cullen, Nick Evans, Peter Furtado, Richard Gombrich, Damien Keown, Gay Watson and above all Eddy Canfor-Dumas and Jo Lane. I hasten to add that they all disagreed with some of my emphases – and also with each other! The jewel of Buddhism has many wonderful facets.

To all of the above I express my heartfelt thanks.

AJM
Oxford, 2019

About the Author

Tony Morris is Chair of the Bleddfa Centre for the Creative Spirit and a Trustee of the Oxford Centre for Buddhist Studies. In previous lives he was a director of Théâtre de Complicité, The History Press and Historypin. His writings include *What Do Buddhists Believe?* (Granta Books, 2006) and *Buddhism by Numbers* (Mud Pie, 2019). When not at his desk he goes for very long walks.

Mud Pie Slices

Fresh Angles on Buddhism

Out Now

Buddhism and Pali • Richard Gombrich

Buddhism AND • Gay Watson

Buddhism and the Menopause • Claire O'Brien

Up Next

Buddhism and Football • George Myerson

Buddhism and Walking • Tony Morris

Buddhism and God • Robert M. Ellis

Buddhism and Myth • Vishvapani Blomfield

Buddhism and the Brain • Wendy Lowes

Buddhism and Light • Marian Partington

Buddhism and Computing • Paul Trafford

Mud Pie

'Buddhist Books and Books for Buddhists'

Mud Pie is an independent specialist online publisher, dedicated to showcasing the best in Buddhist writing.

Our lead title, *The Buddha, Geoff and Me*, has sold over 100,000 copies worldwide.

Contact us at:
www.mudpiebooks.com

Printed in Great
Britain
by Amazon